T0195714

TRANSFORMATION
IN THE MIDST OF
TRANSITION

How to Prosper from Your Storms

CLEVELAND RAMSEY

WESTBOW
PRESS®
A DIVISION OF THOMAS NELSON
& ZONDERVAN

Copyright © 2017 Cleveland Ramsey.

All rights reserved. No part of this book may be used or reproduced by any means, graphic, electronic, or mechanical, including photocopying, recording, taping or by any information storage retrieval system without the written permission of the author except in the case of brief quotations embodied in critical articles and reviews.

Scripture quotations are taken from the King James Version of the Bible.

This book is a work of non-fiction. Unless otherwise noted, the author and the publisher make no explicit guarantees as to the accuracy of the information contained in this book and in some cases, names of people and places have been altered to protect their privacy.

WestBow Press books may be ordered through booksellers or by contacting:

WestBow Press
A Division of Thomas Nelson & Zondervan
1663 Liberty Drive
Bloomington, IN 47403
www.westbowpress.com
1 (866) 928-1240

Because of the dynamic nature of the Internet, any web addresses or links contained in this book may have changed since publication and may no longer be valid. The views expressed in this work are solely those of the author and do not necessarily reflect the views of the publisher, and the publisher hereby disclaims any responsibility for them.

Any people depicted in stock imagery provided by Thinkstock are models, and such images are being used for illustrative purposes only. Certain stock imagery © Thinkstock.

ISBN: 978-1-9736-0077-0 (sc)
ISBN: 978-1-9736-0076-3 (hc)
ISBN: 978-1-9736-0078-7 (e)

Library of Congress Control Number: 2017913336

Print information available on the last page.

WestBow Press rev. date: 10/21/2017

CONTENTS

DEDICATION

—————— ✦ ——————

I dedicate this book to my loving wife, Sharell, my two daughters, Clerell and Clevica, and my son, Cleveland Ramsey Jr. You have been my greatest inspiration and support during the long hours I spent writing this book. Thank you for giving me the time to write and for your kind words of encouragement and prayers during the many storms we have weathered together.

Life can be cold and heartless. Sometimes, trials can knock us down unexpectedly and leave us vulnerable, bleeding, naked, and exposed. At times like those, we have to look to God to transform, refine, and renew our minds so we can emerge stronger and wiser.

We all will have a time of transition when God gives us the opportunity to develop our character, strengthen our faith, and improve our relationship with Him.

ACKNOWLEDGMENTS

I thank the almighty God for giving me the opportunity, wisdom, knowledge, and understanding to complete this project. To God be all the glory for the many great things He has done.

I thank my wife and three children for their consistent support, love, and prayers during the time I spent writing. Their understanding and support have motivated me and kept me inspired to bring this book to fruition.

I extend special thanks to my mentors and senior pastors, Apostle Phalmon Ferguson and Lady Sophia Ferguson, for their dedicated and loving leadership, and to all the members of my church family—United Faith Ministries International.

I thank the entire community of Great Harbor Cay and Bullocks Harbor in the pristine Berry Islands, the Bahamas, for the many transformational experiences God is now using for His glory.

FOREWORD

Apostle Phalmon Ferguson
Senior Pastor, United Faith Ministries International

I am honored to have been asked to write the foreword for such a life-changing book, which was birthed out of a traumatic experience.

Transformation In The Midst of Transition finally, a masterpiece that will teach us how to embrace storms and trials as agents of God's refining process used for developing our lives. This book is filled with deep nuggets that will help individuals who are searching for answers to life's complexing questions. Further, I believe the reader will walk away with a deeper understanding of how to soar like an eagle when facing trials and dust living a purpose driven life.

The author Cleveland Ramsey is a long-time educator in the Commonwealth of the Bahamas who has taught and mentored hundreds of students who are young productive people in our Nation and abroad. His vast experience in the education field makes him a qualified and well able author.

I am so grateful to Pastor Cleveland Ramsey for being led by the Holy Spirit to write such a timely resource book. I am indeed so proud of this remarkable achievement in your life as my spiritual son and pastor. I also wish to congratulate you and your dear family who have supported you through your transition to greatness. Certainly, I believe this book will impact and change a generation of people in years to come. May this book be the beginning of many more to come!

Get ready now for a life-changing journey as you explore each page of this masterpiece!

INTRODUCTION

I have lived long enough and have experienced much that brought me to the sobering reality that believers' problems are often the divine vehicles God uses to transition them into a new season of spiritual growth and promotion. The wrongs unjustly perpetuated on them miraculously work for their good.

We Christians are naturally often perplexed and distressed by the many storms, trials, and fires we encounter daily, but God wants us to understand that our trials are preparing and positioning us for our next level of blessings; they are necessary prerequisites for the new season about to come. How we master our todays will determine how we respond to our tomorrows.

In our storms are numerous hidden blessings; if we appreciate, digest, and evaluate them, we will discover our storms can easily transition us closer to our purposes and destinies.

Transformation in the Midst of Transition teaches you how to

- embrace the benefits and opportunities of your storms by allowing them to transform and transition you to a new level of spiritual growth and development,
- utilize them as a coaching guide to help you navigate effectively through the contemptuous storms and fiery trials of life,
- appreciate the lessons of your past and understand there is more to your life than what you are currently going through by encouraging you to focus rather on where and what God is taking you to,
- manage the new devils at your new levels,
- survive and prosper from your storms,
- comprehend that your storms were designed with your maturity in mind, and
- analyze the storms in your life and how to discover the purpose of each.

God designed your trials to mature and refine you, so do not run away from them or allow yourself to react impulsively before the intended purpose of the storms is accomplished. They will get you to another level where you will learn to praise God even in the midst of the storms. When you look back, you will realize that your storms were designed with your maturity in mind. You will learn how to give God thanks in all your circumstances knowing you will come out better when you were tempted to be bitter.

Friend, God has a divine purpose for every storm you encounter. If your troubles do not kill you, they can bless you. God will use your troubles to advance you, so do not develop a negative attitude and allow your hard days to stagnate your praise. Allow God to get His glory out of all you go through; if He brings it to you, He is awesome enough to bring you through it.

God usually uses trials and storms to unfold His divine plan for His children. In His fatherly way, He summons and allows the appropriate challenges and circumstances to enter our paths that are often pregnant with the potential for spiritual, economic, and emotional growth. These trials are often majestically orchestrated, artistically designed, and uniquely tailored to surgically remove the flesh of the old man so the new man can prosper and mature spiritually.

My wife is an amazing cook. I enjoy watching her plan and execute meals in the kitchen. When she is baking, she makes a list of all the ingredients with the amounts she needs and very meticulously adds them at the right time. Likewise, God knows exactly what we need and when we need it so His result for our lives is fulfilled and our faith develops and strengthens and we transition to our new season. He knows what temperature we need to exist in so authentic transformation will occur.

We ought to embrace this transformation and take responsibility for our spiritual growth so we can be transitioned into our new season. The essential characteristics are to be developed and refined so our new seasons can be introduced; there will be no social promotions for us, my friends.

Transformation in the Midst of Transition encourages and prepares you to embrace your spiritual journey by allowing God's transformative power to process and position you for what is ahead. God's Word has assured us our future is greater than our past. Enjoy the journey, and allow your storms to take you there.

CHAPTER 1

...────ꙮ────...

UNDERSTANDING YOUR
TRANSFORMATION PROCESS—
I AM IN TRANSITION!

I grew up in the Cove, Cat Island, Bahamas. As a boy, I was fascinated by the natural beauty and uniqueness of nature. In addition to feeling drawn to the rolling hills, diverse natural resources, pristine beaches, and captivating historical sites, I was intrigued by the splendid colors of the butterflies that graced the balmy hilltops during long, lazy summer days there.

The processes and biological stages through which those butterflies passed before their emergence in grace and beauty did not concern me—an inquisitive little boy—at the time. Their ugliness during their transformation processes would have been uninviting, boring, and unattractive to my childhood sensibilities; I just saw the result and was fascinated by their radiant beauty.

In retrospect, I have come to see that many believers are like caterpillars that must go through transformation processes during which they do not look attractive, appealing, or even spiritual. You may prefer the result just as I did—the mature butterfly rather than its earlier forms.

Going through to Get To

Just as a beautiful butterfly does not acquire its beauty overnight, our spiritual beauty does not just happen. We are often quick to desire the final product with very little consideration of the processes that produced it. Where we are in our spiritual walk with God did not simply happen; it took time, change, transformation, resources, a nurturing environment, encouragement, correction, direction, assessment, evaluation, breaking, repairing, shaping, molding, restoring, repositioning, refreshing, edifying, sanctifying, teaching, learning, and refining just to name a few of the essential steps.

Before we can enjoy floating through the many corridors of life arrayed majestically in our coats of many colors, we must go through some things to get to where God desires us to be. Our spiritual metamorphosis start with the sobering reality that we all need God, who can transform and transition us to the place where we can pursue our destinies. We all need a holy God to shape and mold us into purposeful soldiers ready for any battle. "And be not conformed to this world: but be ye transformed by the renewing of your mind, that ye may prove what is that good, and acceptable, and perfect, will of God" (Romans 12:2).

The many struggles you are facing have all been sanctioned by a loving God to produce the best in you. What you are going through is temporary, and God will bring you out of it victoriously. Your processing is usually painful and filled with lonely days, sleepless nights, stormy seas, and unpredictable challenges, but they are necessary for your growth and development. Your cocoon stages are often absent of friends to encourage you, but the Lord Himself is your peace right in the middle of your storm. My friend, you must keep on striving even when your plans do not go as you intended. Just remember that these trials often persist because God has a better plan and purpose for your life. "For I know the thoughts that I think toward you, saith the LORD, thoughts of peace, and not of evil, to give you an expected end" (Jeremiah 29:11).

God sees the gold and the good in you, and He wants the best for you. The intensity of the fire you are going through is just a reminder that God is still working on you. He is purifying all that concerns you, and the heat is divinely appointed to destroy all that is artificial so the authentic you can surface as a dynamic, productive, effective, and holy vessel positioned for battle.

Your Good Friday may be difficult, but hang in there because your Sunday morning will come. God will supply the resurrection power so you can rise from any tomb in which your enemies have locked you. Be patient when you are going through what you must go through to receive the blessings your new season will bear like a pregnant woman awaiting the birth of her baby.

Grow Up to Go Up

As a former educator, I am painfully aware of one of the many unfortunate, outdated tragedies in education—children are often promoted from one grade to the next without any consideration of their mastery of what the next grade requires. The age and the number of times the child would have repeated that grade are regularly used as justification for the decision to move him or her along to the next grade. By no means am I an expert in educational psychology, but it never made much sense to me to promote children knowingly when they did not meet a grade's basic requirements. This practice has been one of the contributing factors that have haunted many developing countries socially, economically, and educationally and has led to so many children graduating without basic skills for employment.

I am so happy that in God's kingdom, we have to grow up to go up; there is no social promotion in the kingdom. As believers, we have been challenged to be changed and have our minds renewed daily. We should always be evolving, maturing, learning, growing, strengthening, and transforming ourselves.

> I beseech you therefore, brethren, by the mercies of God, that ye present your bodies a living sacrifice, holy, acceptable unto God, which is your reasonable service. And be not conformed to this world: but be ye transformed by the renewing of your mind, that ye may prove what is that good, and acceptable, and perfect, will of God. For I say, through the grace given unto me, to every man that is among you, not to think of himself more highly than he ought to think; but to think soberly, according as God hath dealt to every man the measure of faith. (Romans 12:1–3)

Believers' characters ought to be changed so they can appreciate the blessings of the new season. Their duties are directed to the desires of the Lord, not this world. They ought to give their bodies willingly to God and keep them unspotted by the world. Those who are transformed are better able to manage the blessings of the next season.

Believers ought to realize that where they are now is not where God destines them to be, that their new seasons will be inaugurated only after they have mastered all their current season presents them. They can expect no social promotion because their next season needs the prerequisite skills they will develop in the current season. God has directed their many setbacks and setups, heartaches and pains, victories and battles, and hills and valleys to work together for their good.

Friend, dry your tears, wash your face, comb your hair, iron your clothes, dress up, and show up to tell the devil you are pressing your way through this storm to get to your destiny. Destiny is calling you higher, but you must prepare yourself during this season to embrace the next season.

Not everyone can go with us as we transition to our new seasons. Our blessings are often delayed because of our choices of companions. God wants to bless us in such a way that no one can claim glory over what He has done, is doing, and will do in our lives. In His wisdom, God prepares us regularly and meticulously in isolation for our coming blessings.

Preparation in Isolation

God puts you on hold not to punish you but to transform your thinking, refine your character, train you, develop your leadership skills, and teach you how to depend on Him alone for provision, protection, and direction. You need to purge your dependence on a worldly system and reprogram it to reflect God's purposes.

I learned to embrace my process and come to the sobering reality that God purposefully hides me so He can prepare me.

We as believers are often well intentioned, but God sees our characters are not yet prepared to manage the abundance of blessings our new season has in store for us that will enable us to survive and cope with adversity. He isolates us so we can train for the many battles He sees ahead. Our responsibility is not to fight the process but embrace our transition, seek God's face, and learn the critical lessons our current season presents.

Too often, we believers develop negative and cancerous attitudes when our challenges become unbearable and life does not go the way we intended. Rather than seeking God's guidance, we frequently resort to doing things our own way, relying on our education and experience to propel us through. Meanwhile, God is jealously waiting for our attention.

When you seek God first, you will soon realize what you are going through is only preparation for what God is taking you to. Your bad days are just making room for your good days, you go through setbacks to get to your comebacks, and your disappointments are making divine appointments for your visit with destiny. Your period of transition may look like a cocoon, but it will get better. Just like the butterfly, you will emerge arrayed majestically in your coat of many colors to become what God intends you to be.

> David therefore departed thence, and escaped to the cave Adullam: and when his brethren and all his father's house heard it, they went down thither to him. And every one that was in distress, and every one that was in debt, and every one that was discontented, gathered themselves unto him; and he became a captain over them: and there were with him about four hundred men. And David went thence to Mizpeh of Moab: and he said unto the king of Moab, Let my father and my mother, I pray thee, come forth, and be with you, till I know what God will do for me. And he brought them before the king of Moab: and they dwelt with him all the while that David was in the hold. (1 Samuel 22:1–4)

This story highlights one of the lowest periods of David's life. He had killed his giant, been anointed king, and was victorious in battle and celebrated, but he was on the run for his life. Many times, what we encounter in life can make or break us. David understood that he was anointed, but before he was to be appointed, he had to master his Adullam; he had to learn valuable lessons, be tested to see if he could be trusted, and mature as a leader in spite of the unpleasantness, inconvenience, and seeming hopelessness his circumstances presented.

I had to come to the realization that God was ultimately in control and that how He processed me was none of my business. I am the clay in the supreme hands of the master Potter, who knows exactly what shaping, shaving, molding, and transforming I need. My responsibility is to trust Him completely with the process that He has ordained for my life by submitting myself humbly and respectfully to whatever He desires for me.

God alone knows what is best for us; He alone knows what is necessary to transform His children into spiritual butterflies He desires. Just as David had, we have the responsibility to do the following during our time of transition when God takes us away from the public eye.

- train and season as leaders
- meet the needs of others God sends us in spite of our circumstances
- trust God to provide for us
- seek God for the lessons He wants us to learn.
- ask God to examine what is really in our hearts.
- let God deal with our player-haters
- remember that God has us and it's not over
- remember that our destinies are secured

You Are in Transition

Your period of transition will make you realize you are not the same person you used to be. The influential friends who were once inseparable and unavoidable parts of your life do not occupy your time and interest anymore. Places that commanded your presence just do not excite you anymore, and the situations that would once leave you upset, confused, and frustrated do not affect you like that anymore. Controversial and debatable issues that once captivated your time, attention, and unthoughtful responses just do not cause you to respond anymore.

You see life through a new pair of spiritual glasses as you mature as a leader and transition into your new season. The big picture of life becomes your priority—having an intimate relationship with God. You realize nothing in life supersedes your spiritual well-being. You methodically become more purpose driven, and you value God's gift of time.

When you reflect on your life, you come to understand that your bad days were just incubators used by God to usher in your good days. Your stormy days were your spiritual gymnasium that God used to prepare and train you so you could live victoriously.

Embracing the Benefits of the Process

God alone knows your destiny, so He strategically designs a process that will surgically cut away the flesh in you so you can fulfill His divine plan for your life and transform you into that special, elite-force soldier prepared for battle.

Our responsibility is to submit to the process and not try to abort, despise, trivialize, or abandon it. We should embrace our transformation processes even though that is painful at times; we should trust God to work out everything for our good (Romans 8:28). We are therefore to submit willingly to God and allow Him to sustain us, fast with expectancy, pray reverently, celebrate others' successes, and leave the player-haters to God. Our battles are not ours; they belong to God, so we should let Him fight them His way.

> Even the youths shall faint and be weary, and the young
> men shall utterly fall: But they that wait upon the Lord
> shall renew their strength; they shall mount up with wings
> as eagles; they shall run, and not be weary; and they shall
> walk, and not faint. (Isaiah 40:30–31)

Transformation can be a very painful and lonely process, but believers have been given the key to success—the ability to be patient until God revives their strength. Just like the eagle, we too will emerge refined, refreshed, and strengthened after we have submitted to the process and allowed it to accomplish what God intended.

> No weapon that is formed against thee shall prosper; and
> every tongue that shall rise against thee in judgment thou
> shalt condemn. This is the heritage of the servants of the

Lord, and their righteousness is of me, saith the Lord. (Isaiah 54:17)

For our light affliction, which is but for a moment, worketh for us a far more exceeding and eternal weight of glory. (2 Corinthians 4:17)

A Time of Spiritual Rejuvenation

Your transition is a time of renewal, reflection, and introspection about who and what you are in God. It is a time to acknowledge that God sees the best in you and desires the best for you. It is a time to get up, dress up, and show up for the battle by allowing God's Word to transition you into your destiny cognizant that He has you covered from all weapons formed against you.

The enemy may try to take the credit for the storms in your life, but I challenge you to stop giving him credit for what God is trying to do in, through, and for you. Shake yourself loose, dust off your despondency, and remind yourself God sanctioned you to get trapped in the net and allowed the enemy to ride over your head but will deliver you to a wealthy place.

> For thou, O God, hast proved us: thou hast tried us, as silver is tried. Thou broughtest us into the net; thou laidst affliction upon our loins. Thou hast caused men to ride over our heads; we went through fire and through water: but thou broughtest us out into a wealthy place. (Psalm 66:10–12)

When we fully comprehend the purpose and power of our storms, we are strengthened by the trials we encounter. James instructed believers to be joyful when their trials came. Job told us to have faith and trust in God even though He may slay us. Paul encouraged us to forget the trials and storms and focus on the future by pressing toward the mark. Jesus reminded believers they were to love and forgive those who did them wrong.

A Time of Character Formation and Sanctification

One of the fundamental purposes of your transition is to help kill the flesh in you. Your next level in God depends on the suffocation of your flesh so you can live. God wants to resurrect you, but there is no accommodation or toleration of one's flesh at your next level. In His wisdom, God often summons particular storms and challenges to help usher you into your next season and purge you of the old flesh that is in your new season. My friend, your flesh is certain to get you in trouble. God wants to glorify in your life, and He will not tolerate your old nature. Your flesh will distract you from your divine assignment and make you focus on your desires rather than the things of God.

> But if the Spirit of him that raised up Jesus from the dead dwell in you, he that raised up Christ from the dead shall also quicken your mortal bodies by his Spirit that dwelleth in you. Therefore, brethren, we are debtors, not to the flesh, to live after the flesh. For if ye live after the flesh, ye shall die: but if ye through the Spirit do mortify the deeds of the body, ye shall live. For as many as are led by the Spirit of God, they are the sons of God. (Romans 8:11–14)

Our goal ought to be to inherit the kingdom of God. Our fleshly tendencies ought to be sacrificed so our fruits of righteousness can be revealed. Our fleshly desires must die because there is no place for negotiation with our flesh. We have been assured, by scripture that if we invest in the flesh, we will reap the benefits of the flesh. The submission of our flesh to God enables the new life of our salvation to become activated in our daily lives. We must allow our flesh to die for the following reasons.

- We are reminded that as believers we do not operate in the flesh any longer (Galatians 2:20, 5:1).
- Believers should live according to the Spirit and forsake the flesh (Galatians 5:16–18).

- Living according to our flesh is carnal and unproductive (Galatians 5:19–21).
- We are unable to delight God while operating in the flesh; it ought to be crucified (Galatians 5:22–26).

You may say you have surrendered your flesh to God, but He is taking His time in coming to see about your situation. Your situation may be stinking to the point that you have hid it in a tomb. You might have requested God's presence; He knew about you yet took His time as He did with Lazarus in coming to address your problem.

The situations of your life may be stinking, but God does not mind that; His concern is your deliverance. It may be ugly, but He can turn your ugliness into beauty. Your situation may also be decomposed and embarrassing, but remember that God specializes in converting a mess into a message, a prison into a palace. This is why He is God, and there is none like Him. He is awesome!

Yes, I know people may have already sung their last song for you and moved on with their lives saying, "It is finished," but friend, it is not the end. Your King is on His way; show Him where you have laid your situation. Never mine others laughing at you; you need a miracle right now, and they do not have any answers for you or for themselves either.

God wants to pronounce life back into your dead, decomposed, and forgotten situation. God wants you to show Him your situations so He can breathe new life into you and resuscitate all that was once dead, stagnant, and ineffective in your life. God wants to resurrect your prayer life and your praise, vision, worship, spirit of excellence, passion, drive, purpose, and testimony.

Despondently, many believers have not experienced the transformative power of their transitions because they have refused to allow God to visit the tombs in which they have buried their dreams over the years of waiting for God to intervene.

As I have on many occasions, you perhaps have done all the stuff that was supposed to be done. We have prayed the right prayers, fasted, and sang the right worship songs, but God takes His time in seeing to our troubles. God often waits for the enemy to have a premature celebration thinking we are finished and our purpose had gone unfulfilled; then He shows up right on time. God's timing is perfect; He knows exactly what we need and when we need it, and He wants the best for us. His plans for our welfare, future, and purpose are assured.

God will get His glory! We believers are to respond to His instructions so our characters will be shaped and formed in His likeness daily. Our struggles are not with flesh and blood but with principalities and other demonic forces in esteemed positions who are on assignment to obliterate our purposes and destinies. We ought to cover ourselves with the armor of God to survive the ferocious and unavoidable attacks (Ephesians 6:11–13).

A Time of Spiritual Resurrection and Transformation

God wants the best for you, nothing less. Let your player-haters hate, let them talk, let them have their celebration over what they assume is your defeat; your Savior is on His way. All you have to do is show Him where you have placed your situation. God wants to resurrect what was dead to new life! Your time of transition is a time for honest introspection and evaluation of where you are in your relationship with God.

Your time of transition is a time for personal reflection and responsibility to mature into that spiritual butterfly God has destined you to be.

- Leave the old you behind (Ephesians 4:17–22).
- Embrace the new you (Ephesians 4:23–29).
- Walk as a child of light (Ephesians 5:13–17).
- Be filled with the Spirit of God (Ephesians 5:18–21).
- Put on the armor of God (Ephesians 6:10–17).

A Time to Demonstrate Love in Our Transitions

Another critical purpose of our times of transition is to sharpen, develop, and show our love for one another. It is easy to point at others while they are being processed because their situations may seem distasteful, ugly, or unsalvageable. Unfortunately, we tend to forget that we too have had our times of ugliness when a merciful God looked down on us favorably and lifted us. We have not always been good, dignified, and pleasant to be around, so we ought to express to others the love God extended to us during our transformation process.

The story of the Good Samaritan reminds us that genuine love is often forgotten when we allow our religious and sanctimonious duties to dominate our Christian responsibility to love. Quite often, we leave each other on the road of life as we pass by assuming someone else will help the wounded soldier even though God has equipped us to lend a helping hand. What if God had passed on the other side of the road to avoid our messy situations?

We should let others know that we may not understand all the processes they are going through but that we will be there to encourage, support, and keep them covered in prayers knowing their change will come.

God Is in Control

The fact that God is in control of all our circumstances is a sobering reality. We do not have to know or understand the details of a storm; we should just believe God is in control of the ship. His character creates comfort, and He is faithful to pilot us through our stormy seas. The weather report is not our business. God will often pause to examine our maturity levels to see if we fully understand He is in control. Our attitude of love in spite of what others may say, do, or think about us is a prerequisite to our breakthroughs.

Understanding that God is ultimately in control gives you the ability and the spiritual stamina to forgive others who have done you wrong. As you transition to your next level, your perspective changes and you acknowledge the fact that no one should have the power over you where you cannot forgive that individual. As you transition into your blessings, God will give you the strength to lay aside all weight and sin so you can have the unction to function in your new season and the ability to allow your past to be just that—your past.

Key Points to Remember

- ✓ Transformation is uncomfortable but necessary.
- ✓ One must be willing to go through to get to where God wants you to be.
- ✓ Grow up to go up.
- ✓ Transformation can be a very painful and lonely process, but believers have received the key for success, which is to wait and be patient until God revives their strength.
- ✓ Your isolation is for your preparation.
- ✓ When God puts you on hold, it is not to punish you but to transform your thinking, refine your character, train you, develop your leadership skills, and teach you how to depend on Him alone for provision, protection, and direction.
- ✓ We should embrace our process even though that is painful at times, and we should trust God that all we experience is working together in harmony for our good.
- ✓ Your process will transform you into that special soldier prepared for battle.
- ✓ Submit to your process with the right attitude.
- ✓ Transition is a time for spiritual rejuvenation.
- ✓ The enemy may try to take the credit for the storms in your life, but I challenge you to stop giving him credit for what God is trying to do in you, through you, and for you.
- ✓ God in His wisdom often summons the right storms and challenges to help usher you into your next season and purge you of the old flesh that is unwelcome in your new season.
- ✓ Your time of transition is a time for honest introspection and evaluation of where you are in your relationship with God.
- ✓ Transition is a time for character formation and sanctification.
- ✓ Transition is a time to master the power of love.
- ✓ God is still in control regardless of what life may throw at you.
- ✓ God's character creates comfort, and He will faithfully navigate you through all stormy seas.

.... ❧ ....

CHAPTER 2

THE TRANSFORMATIONAL POWER OF FORGIVENESS— ALLOWING YOUR PAST TO BE YOUR PAST

Believers' transformation processes are incomplete if they do not address the unforgiveness in their hearts. Most of us have festering emotional wounds we have not forgiven. As God transitions us, and renews our minds, He will reveal persons or situations that have caused or are causing uneasiness, pain, or spiritual discomfort. This discomfort is usually a direct indicator of an area in our lives that needs wholeness and healing. This is all a part of the transforming process that involves renewing our minds as we make our transitions. Unforgiveness stagnates spiritual growth and hinders our ability to transition to the next level of maturity in Christ.

The transformational power of forgiveness demands that unclosed doors of your past close conscientiously so your past can finally be your past. Too many believers are still handcuffed to the hurts, pains, and unpleasant experiences of their past and cannot fully appreciate the joy and beauty of their present circumstances. The strongholds of the past can enslave believers to reliving their failures rather than embracing the opportunities of their future to grow and mature into all God has destined them to be.

Not as though I had already attained, either were already perfect: but I follow after, if that I may apprehend that for which also I am apprehended of Christ Jesus. Brethren, I count not myself to have apprehended: but this one thing I do, forgetting those things which are behind, and reaching forth unto those things which are before, I press toward the mark for the prize of the high calling of God in Christ Jesus. (Philippians 3:12–14)

God is calling His people to officiate at the home going ceremony of their pasts. He anointed and appointed His people to declare dust-to-dust, ashes to ashes over their hurts and pains. It may be situations from childhood that were unaddressed by those who should have gotten help rather than hide behind the "Child, just pray about it" syndrome. By no means am I underestimating the power of prayer, but we all know that after praying, we often have to do something for ourselves—rise and walk.

Release the Pain of the Past so It Will Not Overwhelm You

Wherefore seeing we also are compassed about with so great a cloud of witnesses, let us lay aside every weight, and the sin which doth so easily beset us, and let us run with patience the race that is set before us, Looking unto Jesus the author and finisher of our faith; who for the joy that was set before him endured the cross, despising the shame, and is set down at the right hand of the throne of God. For consider him that endured such contradiction of sinners against himself, lest ye be wearied and faint in your minds. (Hebrews 12:1–3)

God Wants You to Be Happy and Live an Accomplished Life

The thief cometh not, but for to steal, and to kill, and to destroy: I am come that they might have life, and that they might have it more abundantly. (John 10:10)

God Wants to Take Your Pain; Let Him Have It

> Come unto me, all ye that labour and are heavy laden, and
> I will give you rest. Take my yoke upon you, and learn of
> me; for I am meek and lowly in heart: and ye shall find
> rest unto your souls. (Matthew 11:28–29)

The Struggle Is Real

Many believers have prayed, but our guilt, memories, pain, anger,
bitterness, and frustration remain. Many of us have not had effective spiritual
counselling to know how to live healthy and productive lives by allowing
God to use our pain for His glory. Many of us have not learnt how to declare
what God said concerning our situations rather than what we thought, felt,
or imagined. Many believers struggle with wounds of their pasts and love
the Lord, but they do not know how to let go of their pain in a healthy way
to prevent their issues from affecting their ministries and destinies.

Your destiny is depending on your willingness to look at the hurts of
your past honestly and by allowing God to utilize your pain to propel you
into your destiny. God uses your pain to usher in your purpose. Your pain
should work for your gain, and there is purpose wrapped up in your pain!

It Is Okay to Hurt

There is nothing wrong with being hurt and wounded; Christ was, and
you will too. Believers must come to grips with the reality that being hurt
is an integral part of life. People, situations, and circumstances will often
cause pain and disappointment. They ought to find a way to allow their
pain to propel them toward their destinies. The hurt and pain believers
experience is often not about them personally but about their destinies
and the fulfillment of God's purpose. Their focus should be on the critical
messages and lessons God is revealing through the tribulation.

> He is despised and rejected of men; a man of sorrows, and
> acquainted with grief: and we hid as it were our faces from

him; he was despised, and we esteemed him not. Surely he hath borne our griefs, and carried our sorrows: yet we did esteem him stricken, smitten of God, and afflicted. But he was wounded for our transgressions, he was bruised for our iniquities: the chastisement of our peace was upon him; and with his stripes we are healed. (Isaiah 53:3–5)

Then said Jesus, Father, forgive them; for they know not what they do. And they parted his raiment, and cast lots. (Luke 23:34)

Blessed be God, even the Father of our Lord Jesus Christ, the Father of mercies, and the God of all comfort; Who comforteth us in all our tribulation, that we may be able to comfort them which are in any trouble, by the comfort wherewith we ourselves are comforted of God. (2 Corinthians 1:3–4)

Let Your Past Be Your Past

What happened in our past is just that, our past. Our spiritual transformation has produced new creatures. Believers ought to realize that our failures and pains cannot dictate, abort, or cancel the purposes of God for our lives. Our focus then ought to be on learning lessons from the past and applying them to our lives as God transitions us to the next level.

Allowing past failures to dominate our lives to the extent of paralyzing our testimony indicates a lack of understanding of God's grace. The love and mercy He shows to us ought to be noticeable in how we extend mercy to others. Our testimonies should be about how God delivered, showed mercy, transformed, repositioned, and transitioned us notwithstanding our shortcomings.

Therefore if any man be in Christ, he is a new creature: old things are passed away; behold, all things are become new. (2 Corinthians 5:17)

Nevertheless when it shall turn to the Lord, the vail shall be taken away. Now the Lord is that Spirit: and where the Spirit of the Lord is, there is liberty. But we all, with open face beholding as in a glass the glory of the Lord, are changed into the same image from glory to glory, even as by the Spirit of the Lord. (2 Corinthians 3:16–18)

And be not conformed to this world: but be ye transformed by the renewing of your mind, that ye may prove what is that good, and acceptable, and perfect, will of God. (Romans 12:2)

If so be that ye have heard him, and have been taught by him, as the truth is in Jesus: That ye put off concerning the former conversation the old man, which is corrupt according to the deceitful lusts; And be renewed in the spirit of your mind; And that ye put on the new man, which after God is created in righteousness and true holiness. (Ephesians 4:21–24)

The Pain in Your Past Was Meant for Your Gain

What happened in your past ought to be used to make your life better, not bitter. The challenge for every believer is to allow the Holy Spirit to convert the pain of the past into praise and thanksgiving in the future. What the enemy intended to destroy you with in your past ought to be used as testimony to help encourage others. There is no need to be afraid of your past; just allow God to get His glory out of every area of your life.

- Your past will work for your good (Romans 8:28).
- Divorce the old man and embrace your new man (Ephesians 4:21–24).
- Kill your past daily so your new nature can mature (1 Corinthians 15:30–31).

- Do not fear your past because the Lord called you when others refused you (Isaiah 54:4–6).
- Jesus has been nailed your past to the cross, so leave it there (Colossians 2:13–14).

The Benefits of Forgiveness in the Pursuit of Destiny

Forgiveness is essential for transformation; you will benefit if you seek forgiveness so the enemy cannot use it to sabotage your future. While you cannot make anyone forgive, your attitude of seeking forgiveness will clear your conscience with God.

The enemy will use any opportunity to thwart the fulfillment of your purpose. He will try to use any unforgiveness to contradict or reduce the impact of your testimony. Do not allow the enemy to use you against yourself. Do not allow him to tell you what you are being directed to do is only your mind talking to you. If God reveals it, deal with it. Due to your new nature in Christ, you possess the power to confront any form of unforgiveness.

Forgive Those Who Have Mistreated You because the Enemy Cannot Stop God's Purpose and Plan for Your Life

> And they sent a messenger unto Joseph, saying, Thy father did command before he died, saying, so shall ye say unto Joseph, Forgive, I pray thee now, the trespass of thy brethren, and their sin; for they did unto thee evil: and now, we pray thee, forgive the trespass of the servants of the God of thy father. And Joseph wept when they spake unto him. And his brethren also went and fell down before his face; and they said, Behold, we be thy servants. (Genesis 50:16–18)

Forgive Those Who Took Advantage of You Financially so God Can Forgive You

Give us this day our daily bread. And forgive us our debts, as we forgive our debtors. And lead us not into temptation, but deliver us from evil: For thine is the kingdom, and the power, and the glory, forever. Amen. (Matthew 6:11–13)

Forgive and Repent of Wicked Ways so God Can Forgive Your Sin and Bring Healing to Your Land

If my people, which are called by my name, shall humble themselves, and pray, and seek my face, and turn from their wicked ways; then will I hear from heaven, and will forgive their sin, and will heal their land. (2 Chronicles 7:14)

Forgive Others so God Can Forgive You

For if ye forgive men their trespasses, your heavenly Father will also forgive you: But if ye forgive not men their trespasses, neither will your Father forgive your trespasses. (Matthew 6:14–15)

Be ye therefore merciful, as your Father also is merciful. Judge not, and ye shall not be judged: condemn not, and ye shall not be condemned: forgive, and ye shall be forgiven. (Luke 6:36–37)

Forgive Others so Your Prayers Can Be Answered

Therefore I say unto you, what things so ever ye desire, when ye pray, believe that ye receive them, and ye shall have them. And when ye stand praying, forgive, if ye ought against any: that your Father also which is in heaven may forgive you your trespasses. But if ye do not forgive, neither will your Father which is in heaven forgive your trespasses. (Mark 11:24–26)

God Will Forgive Those Who Confess Their Sins

If we say that we have no sin, we deceive ourselves, and the truth is not in us. If we confess our sins, he is faithful and just to forgive us our sins, and to cleanse us from all unrighteousness. If we say that we have not sinned, we make him a liar, and his word is not in us. (1 John 1:8–10)

Vengeance Belongs to God

The Lord revealed to me that I had former colleagues at a job in public service who were upset with me for the speedy and unexpected way I had departed. Over the years, we had developed a close bond, and my sudden exit had affected them in many ways that were not evident or of any real concern to me when I left. I knew what I did was the right thing to do for me to pursue my destiny, but was later reminded by the Lord that I had to address that situation and seek forgiveness for having inadvertently hurt them.

As you transition to your next level, periodically God will make you aware about the pain you have unintentionally caused others. The enemy, to prevent you from pursuing your destiny can use that pain that is unaddressed, as a stronghold. My friend, it is always wise to seek forgiveness from those you have offended as soon as you can. Your destiny demands that you put off every weight that can delay or deny you the blessings of your destiny. The pursuance of your divine purpose and destiny are essential for your existence, and nothing should be left unaddressed that opposes the plans and purposes of God.

As believers, we can find it easy to accept God's forgiveness, the forgiveness of others who have done us wrong, and of those persons, we have wronged. Unfortunately, the challenge comes when we have to forgive ourselves! We can keep ourselves from maximizing our potential when we do not release ourselves from the hurt of our past so God can give us the strength to embrace our future.

Many times, I wanted revenge on those who had wronged me. Life sometimes seems so unfair, but when we reflect on all the wrong we have done ourselves, we become reinvigorated to praise God in spite of our perplexities and insecurities.

As a young man, I struggled with the pain of not being able to address situations in the manner I thought was appropriate. Thank God, for my dearly departed mother, Mrs. Olive Arlean Ramsey, who intervened regularly and right in time and reminded me rather strongly that vengeance belonged to God. I rationalized that since created in His image; I had the right to assist Him with the execution of justice on those I thought deserved it. As I matured, I realized that I too was not perfect and needed forgiveness from God and others for my many shortcomings.

As a husband, father, community leader, businessperson, and minister, I understand now that it is easy to offend unintentionally in my daily walk. Forgiveness is essential so we do not have to live with the guilt and weight of unforgiveness. Our willingness to forgive quickly and honestly should always be our priority. I am not suggesting we should not hurt because that is normal and healthy to do, but we should always accept God's command as supreme and forgive unconditionally. It is critical and necessary for our own ability to have forgiveness from our heavenly Father.

Forgiveness Releases the Pain

The tendency not to forgive can feed the desire to seek revenge for the pain we are experiencing. Forgiveness releases the pain and tells us psychologically that it is okay to heal. We must release ourselves from the bondage that can accompany pain. Failure to do so can create a foundation on which the enemy builds a stronghold to manipulate our decisions. Forgiveness does not mean we will forget past pain and injustices perpetrated on us, but it liberates us from allowing the pain to delay our destinies.

Tragically, many people have made terrible decisions in their family lives that attributed to the unforgiveness they carried from their youth involving dysfunctional relationships with their parents. The much dysfunction in our homes today has a direct relation to the inability or unwillingness to confront the pain of past hurtful situations experienced by various family members.

Subsequently, many have busied themselves pursuing success in the hopes of medicating the pain with successful endeavors. Unfortunately, many will soon wake up and despondently discover that something is still missing. They should address that void to develop a real appreciation for whose they are and for what they have become. Recognize their pain, accept it, and the impact it is having or has had on their lives. They must confront it in a healthy, methodical manner with a view to bringing about emotional, psychological, and spiritual healing before it can be used to propel them toward their destinies.

Adopting the Right Attitude

Job prayed for his friends who questioned his relationship with God and self-righteously assumed he had sinned based on the severity of his troubles (Job 42). Miraculously, his blessings were released after he prayed for his enemies, and God turned his situation around that all those who once despised him had to come and be a blessing to him. Often, God is observing our maturity level to see if we fully understand that He is in control. Friend, your ability to love in spite of what others say, do, or think about you is usually a prerequisite to your breakthrough.

Your transition is a time for thoughtful introspection about how God had forgiven you when perhaps you did not even do anything to deserve it. Your new level in God has no space for the old, heavy baggage of unforgiveness of your yesterdays. I challenge you to pray for those who have done you wrong.

As I conclude this chapter, I am finishing a seven-day fast during which God dealt with me concerning a matter that had caused me great pain. I did not know how to release myself from the intentional hurt and pain that inflicted me by people I knew in an attempt to destroy my character, ruin my finances, and interrupt my family and ministry. I prayed one night during the fast that God would bless those individuals, allow me to forgive them, and take away the resentment I felt. I told each one, "I release and forgive you in the name of Jesus."

My own attitude frustrated the blessings on my life. Each of us holds the key to our breakthroughs when we harbor unforgiveness in our hearts. Let that player-hater watch how God will prepare us a table in the presence of those who mean us harm. Just like Joseph, we will testify that what intended to destroy us was turned around by God to bless us.

I finally but painfully discovered that my enemies were on assignment to push me into my blessings and destiny. God opened doors that blessed my family financially and spiritually more than we were before. The stress level of a demanding job in my life disappeared; I finally had more time to spend with my family and to study God's Word. My process of affliction was indeed painful and emotionally draining, but God was there working things out in my favor. Job forgave, prayed for his enemies, and got additional blessings. As you forgive and pray for your enemies as Job did, you too will experience how blessings flow when you forgive.

Feeling and accepting your pain is emotionally productive. We believers must submit ourselves to God's will and acknowledge that Christ in us is working through us and giving us the power to forgive. When we do, we start building a stable foundation on which our healing can begin. It is God's will that we seek forgiveness and learn to forgive ourselves.

The unwillingness to forgive yourself can lead to spiritual and emotional stagnation. Let the healing began today as you transition to your next level toward your purpose. Like the Prodigal Son, you must conclude, "There is more to my life than this. I am coming out of this!" You must take responsibility for yourself and decide to go to your Father and leave your pain there.

Key Points to Remember

- ✓ Forgiveness is liberating.
- ✓ Forgiveness is transformational.
- ✓ Forgiveness is a cleansing experience.
- ✓ Forgiveness is healthy and productive.
- ✓ Forgiveness enhances spiritual growth.

✓ Forgiveness is commanded by God.

✓ Forgiveness is not optional with God.

✓ Forgiveness is not forgetfulness.

✓ Forgiveness is Christlike.

✓ Forgiveness is therapeutic.

✓ Forgiveness helps to release your pain.

✓ Forgiveness is beneficial to you.

✓ Forgiveness is possible and within your capabilities.

✓ Forgiveness is critical to your spiritual maturity and development.

✓ Forgiveness is essential if you are to transition to your next level.

✓ Forgiveness is essential to the fulfillment of your purpose and destiny.

CHAPTER 3

---❦---

TRANSFORMATION IN THE PIGPEN— THERE IS MORE TO MY LIFE THAN THIS!

M any of us have found ourselves at times in uncommon places doing unusual things with unfamiliar people. Some believers may find themselves looking at the food meant for pigs thinking they could and should have some. Unfortunately, disobedience to the principles of God can bring us to the point where we encounter what I call a pigpen experience.

Many of us have been to our lowest when we were about to do crazy stuff that had the potential to destroy us and wreck our futures. The good news is that God sees and knows right where we are, and if we trust Him, He will deliver us and create a message from our messes.

I have had many unpleasant experiences where God rescued me just in time before I self-destructed. God in his wisdom continues to use all our experiences—good and bad—to work out His purpose and to direct us back to Him.

The Prodigal Son's revelation came just in time for his deliverance. Many of us have had, or have "pigs" in our lives whose purpose is to remind us of our heritage in our Father's house. Our pigs should never be despised because they can bring us to the reality of our situations and cause us to thoroughly assess where we are, whose we are, why we are, and where we ought to be.

Thank God for Our Pigs

The story of the Prodigal Son is symbolic of many believers who have drifted from the presence, protection, and guidance of the Lord to enjoy life their way. Unfortunately, many find themselves empty of substance and exhausted from unproductive projects, people, and things that did not have an authentic appreciation for the gift or the Giver.

The Prodigal Son discovered that the gifts would soon run out when inappropriately used in disobedience to the Giver and ungodly endeavors. Our blessings should not be abused in the pursuance of anything out of the will of God for our lives. To do so would be blatant disobedience, but thank God, for our pigs that remind us our Father has a greater plan for our lives.

Your Pigs Are Not Your Purpose

The pigpen experience opened the Prodigal Son's eyes; he realized he had made a great mistake in his youthful judgment. The pigs' food reminded him of his heritage as a son in the kingdom of God. God specializes in using the simple to reveal to us the profound mysteries of His kingdom. The pigs' food activated his spiritual senses and reignited a passion for life. He surmised, "There is more to my life than this! These pigs are not my purpose! I am coming out of this!"

The pigpen experience I encountered served as a mirror that reflected the real me. It caused me to ask myself the tough questions and realize my life meant more than what I was experiencing. I came to the painful realization that my pigs served a valuable purpose—they got me back where I belonged. They can be a reflector of where you are in relation to your destiny. What is your mirror? Do you like what you see? What will you do now that you know what is on the inside? The Prodigal Son saw his purpose, potential, and opportunity.

Amazingly, God quite regularly allows situations to come your way so you can come to yourself as the Prodigal Son did. Some smelly and unpleasant situations may come your way, but they will reflect who you really are. You may have gotten yourself into your pigpen through disobedience, impatience, or arrogance, but God's love is so great that He will protect you from harm and danger even in your pigpens.

The purpose for our lives surpasses our human imperfections and spiritual ignorance. Mud may be on us, but thank God, it is not in us. We must wise up and acknowledge our Father is a King and we are royalty. There is more to our lives than this. We are special, and there is purpose in us. We must arise, shake ourselves off, dry our tears and wipe our eyes, straighten up, tell those pigs goodbye, and go home to our Father (Luke 15:11–20).

The Transformation Process

The Prodigal Son experienced a spiritual transformation; his life could not remain the same. Changes were imminent, and his pigs became his transformational mirror that caused him to see himself as he was. What he saw was not what he knew ought to have been there. He painfully discovered he was out of the position, presence, provision, and protection of his Father's love.

Friend, you too may come to the point in your life when you know where you are currently is not where you were destined to be. Your revelation that you are out of position ought to propel you to take the following steps to return to the Father.

Acknowledge You Are Out of Position

God sometimes allows situations He designs to cause you to see where you are: "He came to himself" (Luke 15:17). The Prodigal Son realized he was in the pigpen but was not *of* the pigpen; it was not his destiny or home. His spiritual DNA was different; he could not digest the food the pigs ate even if he tried. Your pigs are not your purpose, and your process is not your purpose—your purpose is at home where you belong.

God wants us to acknowledge where we are in Christ, and my friend, it is not over until God says it is over. We serve a pick-me-up God able to turn our bad situations around so we can serve Him. He wants to wash us of the mud and purify us with His blood, which can turn our dark and hopeless situations around just in time.

He can

- take you from your pit to your prison and from your prison to your palace. Just ask Joseph.
- convert your sorrow to joy and give you more than double for your trouble. Just ask Job.
- stand with you in your fiery furnace, insulate you from the fire, and allow you to come out without even smelling like smoke or whatever you have been in or through. Just ask the three Hebrew boys.
- send an earthquake to rescue you from your imprisonment and turn your prison into a revival service. Ask Paul and Silas.
- send an angel to rescue you from the claws of the enemy when they have plans to kill you. Ask Peter.
- turn a murderer into a deliverer. Ask Moses.
- turn an unrecognized little shepherd boy into a giant killer. Ask David.
- Turn your mess into a message to reach and bless many. Just ask me!

My friend, we serve an awesome and mighty God who does not need anyone's permission to qualify the unqualified and use whom and what others may have despised. The Bible contains several characters rejected by humanity but used by God. Your pitfalls on the way to your destiny are often pregnant with opportunities for achieving spiritual maturity.

Conduct an Honest Assessment and Inventory of Where You Are

God wants us to do spiritual assessments of where we are and compare them to where we are supposed to be. The Prodigal Son remembered that his home was better than where he was and that he had a father who loved him. There comes a point in our lives that we must realize we can do better.

The son acknowledged that his father had bread enough to spare and that there was no reason why he had to be in the condition he was in that had resulted from his disobedience, but despite that, he had hope because he was still alive.

As we experience transformation, we must be honest with our relationship with God. We should take inventory of our situations and compare it with what our heavenly Father has to offer.

Ask yourself,

- Is my mind at peace with God?
- Is my behavior and attitude pleasing to God?
- How is my spiritual standing with God?
- Is my spirit at peace with my decision?
- What is my mental condition?
- What is my physical condition?
- What is my social and economic status?
- Who am I?
- Where am I going?
- How will I get there?
- Whom do I belong?
- Do I have God's approval to be where I am?
- How did I arrive where I am?
- Am I better off now than I was before?
- Am I happy?
- Is God proud and pleased with where I am now? Why? Why not?
- Am I pursuing my purpose passionately?

Make a Destiny-Focused Decision and Take Action

We must decide on what action we will take after making a decision to get up and go home. There comes a time in all our lives when we must make a destiny decision that can affect our lives. The Prodigal Son made a decision: "I will arise" (Luke 15:18). He recognized he was in the wrong place with the wrong associates and around the wrong food hoping for a right result. He accepted that this situation was not healthy for his spiritual advancement.

Give the pigs' food to the pigs. It is not helpful for your growth; it will suffocate your spirituality. Your Father has better, and you can enjoy better even as a hired servant.

Taking Responsibility for Your Condition

This wayward son took responsibility for his situation. He did not blame the church, his upbringing, or his ethnicity for his condition. He prophesied to his situation and told himself he was not staying there because there was more to his life than what he was experiencing. We must all learn how to say, "I am coming out of this. There is more to my life than this. This too shall pass. My Father has a better life for me than this."

Tell your pigs goodbye; their purpose is finished. Your transition to your next level is awaiting you. Go back to your Father, who is waiting for you to come home. You may inquire what you need to arise from; I say complacency, laziness, stress, bad friends, destructive habits, irresponsible behavior, unproductive activities, riotous living, and purposeless endeavors. Your time is precious, my friend, and God is expecting you to utilize your time as a valuable resource to fulfill your purpose and to pursue your destiny.

The sad reality is that many of our lives are filled with misery, hopelessness, and unfulfilled dreams because we have refused to leave our pigs and go home. Many families are dysfunctional, and many children are fatherless and motherless because many of us are refusing to go home. Many marriages are in disarray and broken because we are refusing to go home.

The Prodigal Son would have never known his father was waiting patiently and expectantly if he had not gone home. He would never have received his ring, robe, and party had he not gone home. God is waiting for His children to come back home.

Choose Your New Destination and Put a Name on It

We must leave our pigpens and pigs and choose a new destination. As believers, we must learn how to verbalize the purpose for our lives. We must learn how to declare the things that concern us before we can see any of our purposes fulfilled. We must always declare what God has said about our situations rather than what others or we think, feel, or imagine. We might be dirty, smelly, tied, busted, disgusted, broke, frustrated, disappointed, hungry, or sick, but we can go home. Every step we take in that direction is a step closer to our purpose and destiny, and our destinies are calling our names.

Do not go to another pigpen; go home, my friend, because your Father is waiting. True repentance is turning away from the pigpen experiences that have distracted you from the real purposes for your life. You must be humble enough to go in the opposite direction—toward improving your life. True repentance is evident in what you do more than in what you say. Your willingness to take corrective action is a reliable indicator of the condition of your repentant heart.

The lost son chose his direction: "And go to my father" (Luke 15:18); you must do the same. Speak to your future and chart your course as you go home. Be specific and deliberate in where you decide to go. Learn to speak prophetically to your future, and call forth what you desire but cannot see in the physical.

My friend, life and death are in the power of the tongue. This is a religious responsibility, and the best decision you can make is to go to your Father, who waits for you. Your repentant heart will birth a change in your spiritual appetite and attitude.

Change Your Attitude

God wants to humble you and change your attitude. Confession is the key to your reconciliation with our Father. The lost son did not give excuses but came out and admitted his wrongdoing: "Father I have sinned" (Luke 15:18). Accept responsibility for what you have done, where you have been, and where you are going.

God loves people who are real and repentant. Repentance is necessary before restoration and reconciliation can take place. A changed mind can propel us quickly to our destinies. We should renew our minds because our greatest battles occur in our minds; whoever wins the battle for our minds has the advantage over us.

Expect Opposition When You Decide to Go to Your Father

Sadly, your greatest oppositions often come from those in your circle who should be rejoicing that you finally made the decision to come home and receive restoration. The enemy knows his impact will be greater if those closest to you cause your resentment. The enemy wants you to forget about the mess you were in, and your deliverance. He wants to focus your attention on the hurt and pain of your present circumstances so you will forget to praise God for what He has done, is doing, and will do. He wants you to get upset about the others who do not celebrate with you.

I have come to the painful understanding that not everyone will be happy you are back at home. Too many persons are resentful over what God is doing in others' lives. Both characters in this story were sons, but the elder son was unwilling to forgive even though his father, who was done wrong, was happy to forgive. It is ironic that God forgives us but we are so reluctant to forgive others who have not even offended us directly.

The seed of unforgiveness can turn into contempt and pride. The elder son refused to heed the invitation of his own father and proclaimed he was not coming to the celebration for his brother. How often we do the same thing—we refuse invitations from the Father because we are envious of another brother or sister's blessing. How do we know our blessings are not next in line? How do we know if the Father was not testing our attitudes just to see if we could celebrate what He is doing in another's life before we receive our own breakthroughs and blessings? How do we know if the Father did not plan to bless and appreciate us at the celebration too? Failure to show up at others' celebrations will disqualify us from ever knowing the intention of the Father. Do not allow your pride to abort your potential blessings.

This older son's resentment led to isolation, and that is where the enemy wants us to be. He manipulates our pride and cunningly tells us we deserve better treatment because of what we have done over the years.

There is no scriptural record to support that the older brother looked for his brother, or tried to discourage him from leaving home in the first place. He seems to be like many believers who are trying to win their way into heaven by their works and not through love. In the absence of love, our Christian walk becomes a duty we carry out for fame and name but not for God. God is love, and He does nothing without love (John 3:16).

The Power of Love in Your Transition

The older brother's lack of love made him cold and heartless; he refused to attend the celebration. Real transformation demands that you forget about how you may be feeling and step out in faith and obedience to trust your Father when He calls you to the party for your returned brother. Your attendance is a direct reflection of your love for your Father and brother.

The bible teaches believers not to look down on others because of what they are going through. We must always realize they belong to God, who is working some stuff out in their lives we may not know about, so we should not judge others; we should just love them. Love prompts us to say, "I do not understand all your process, but I will be here to encourage, support, to keep you covered until your change comes."

Everything God allows to come our way has a purpose. All our pain, shortcomings, and successes are woven together by God to bring out His divine plan and purpose for our lives (Romans 8:28).

This older brother is a metaphor for many in the body of Christ today who refuse to rejoice with their brothers and sisters who have made the life-changing choice to return home to their Father. The Bible makes it clear that heaven rejoices over even just one sinner who comes home.

As matured individuals, we must learn to accept and respect the views of others but not allow their indifference to stop, delay, deny, or abort the celebration our Father has prepared. Do not be intimidated; enjoy the many gifts that were prepared for you.

Attend Your Party with a Grateful Attitude

Enjoy your party and appreciate the fatted calf prepared just for you. God promised to prepare you a table in the presence of your enemies, so stop worrying about those who do not wish to celebrate you and enjoy your blessings.

Friend, even while you were in your pigpen dilemma, your Father was preparing for your return. Your calf made fattened. God wants to celebrate your return to where you belong.

Wear Your Ring with a Humble Heart

Your ring is a sign to you that you were restored to your rightful position. Genuine repentance leads to restoration. You have the authority entrusted to you by your Father that you are able to rebuke and speak to your atmosphere and receive health, wealth, and opportunities.

Cover Yourself with God's Robe of Righteousness

God wants to clothe us with His righteousness and love, so we should wear His covering with grateful hearts and an appreciation for our alienation but now found, blinded by sin but now seeing clearly, dead in sin but now having life, paralyzed by sin but now walking in righteousness. We should put on God's robe of righteousness and wear it with dignity and reverence.

You Are God's Child, so Put on Your Shoes

Put on the shoes God gives you. You requested demotion to being just a servant, but our Father has restored you to your former position. Your Father acknowledged your repentant attitude, and He decided to promote you to the position of a child of God again with tangible evidence for all to see.

What a mighty God we serve! God wants to bless us tangibly so our player-haters can see, feel, touch, hear, smell, and taste His blessings.

Accept your restoration and resume your position, authority, and acceptance in God.

> And we know that all things work together for good to them that love God, to them who are the called according to his purpose. For whom he did foreknow, he also did predestinate to be conformed to the image of his Son, that he might be the firstborn among many brethren. Moreover whom he did predestinate, them he also called: and whom he called, them he also justified: and whom he

justified, them he also glorified. What shall we then say to these things? If God be for us, who can be against us? (Romans 8:28–31)

Come unto me, all ye that labor and are heavy laden and I will give you rest. Take my yoke upon you, and learn of me; for I am meek and lowly in heart: and ye shall find rest unto your souls. For my yoke is easy, and my burden is light. (Matthew 11:28–29)

Hear my cry, O God; attend unto my prayer. From the end of the earth will I cry unto thee, when my heart is overwhelmed: lead me to the rock that is higher than I. For thou hast been a shelter for me, and a strong tower from the enemy. (Psalm 61:1–3)

Make Your Transition Today

Your transformation is for a higher purpose. Your pigpen experience can propel you toward your destiny; it can work for your good. Your purpose is patiently waiting on your return to your Father. Yes, you may be busted, broke, disgusted, frustrated, agitated, tired, and depressed, but God is willing and able to restore everything stolen from you. God is waiting on you to come home. Your focus should always be on where God is taking you rather than the temporary discomfort of what you are going through.

The trials and challenges of our past met approval by God to transition us into our destinies. The good and the bad, the vicissitudes, the hills and valleys, and the highs and the lows of life all are for our good. Our Father is prepared to bless us tangibly and allow our enemies to witness our promotion and elevation as He prepares our table in the presence of our enemies.

Key Points to Remember

- ✓ Disobedience can lead us to unpleasant, embarrassing, unhealthy, and ungodly situations.
- ✓ Do not despise your pigs; they are there to remind you of your purpose.
- ✓ Your pigs are not your purpose.
- ✓ You may be in the pigpen, but you are not of the pigpen.
- ✓ Jesus's blood will cleanse all the pigpen impurities off you.
- ✓ Mud may be on you, but thank God, it is not in you.
- ✓ Realize that where you are is not where you were destined to be.
- ✓ Transition back to your Father because He is waiting for you to come home.
- ✓ You must humble yourself, take action, and reposition yourself where you belong.
- ✓ Enjoy the blessings when you return home.
- ✓ Expect enemies when you decide to go home to fulfill your purpose.
- ✓ Your enemies are often right at home waiting to bring your celebration to disrepute.
- ✓ Accept your blessings and be thankful for your restoration.
- ✓ Put on your ring, robe, and shoes, hold your head high, and enjoy the party your Father has organized for you.
- ✓ Your Sunday morning has come, so arise!
- ✓ Use your many experiences to help pull others out of their pigpens.
- ✓ There is more to your life than what you are going through, so focus on what God is taking you to experience.
- ✓ Remember that God will prepare you a table right in the presence of your enemies.

CHAPTER 4

TRANSFORMATION IN THE MIDST OF ADVERSITY— NEW LEVELS, NEW DEVILS

When God transforms you to your next level, that will attract new devils. Some call them enemies, haters, or jealous folks, but I call them Chaldeans. Your Chaldeans have an assignment to push you away from your destiny. The adversity you experience is only an indicator of the anointing and purpose of God on your life.

The Purpose of Your Chaldeans

The Chaldeans are everywhere—on your job and in church, community, organizations, and even in your family. They will befriend you, but they will then subtly try to destroy your career, character, and means of income. They come in different sizes and at unannounced times and uninformed places. They come in different colors; they are of differing ethnicities, social statuses, and educational levels. They will have mixed religious persuasions and personalities; no one chosen to the body of Christ will go untouched by their influence. I am sure you have several of them who would pat you on the back in the morning and sell you out that evening. They would tell you how excellent you are but then sell you to the highest bidder an hour later. Joseph, Isaac, Job, the three Hebrew boys, Nehemiah, and Jesus Christ all had Chaldeans in their lives, but that was for a greater purpose. If you do not have a few of them in your life, you should question the authenticity of your calling, for you are encouraged by scripture to prepare for the inevitable attacks of the enemy.

> Put on the whole armor of God that ye may be able to stand against the wiles of the devil. For we wrestle not against flesh and blood, but against principalities, against powers, against the rulers of the darkness of this world, against spiritual wickedness in high places. (Ephesians 6:11–12)

> Persecutions, afflictions, which came unto me at Antioch, at Iconium, at Lystra; what persecutions I endured: but out of them all the Lord delivered me. Yea, and all that will live godly in Christ Jesus shall suffer persecution. But evil men and seducers shall wax worse and worse, deceiving, and being deceived. (2 Timothy 3:11–13)

As Christians, we are to maintain a positive attitude toward those who seek our demise. Scriptures admonish us to be courteous and loving to those who seek our destruction knowing that our trust is in God, who will avenge us in His own way and timing. I know that it is very painful to be professional and Christ-like with those church folks, colleagues, associates, and supposedly friends we have helped climb the ladder of success but then find out they are plotting, organizing, and executing a plan to destroy us. In spite of our feelings, we should find ways to raise our hands and thank God for our Chaldeans. The reality is that quite often our enemies can drive us to our knees and cause us to develop a closer walk with God.

Your Chaldeans seek to frustrate your purpose and destiny by attempting to intimidate you from fulfilling God's plan for your life. God is in control; occasionally, He permits the enemy to attack us (Job 1:6–12, 17/ 2:1–10), yet when we are faithful (Job 1:20–22; James 1:12), we are blessed with double for our trouble (Job 42:10–17).

Thank God for Our Chaldeans

Our Chaldeans are often the vehicles God uses to promote us. I know that sounds crazy, unrealistic, and counterproductive, but it is the truth.

The three Hebrew boys experienced their promotion because of the attack of their Chaldeans (Daniel 3:8–18, 26–30).

I know personally the pain of suffering agonizing attacks by Chaldeans who smile in your face with radiant white teeth while they sharpen their long knives in their hearts of jealousy, bitterness, envy, and hatred. I know the chilling pain of the long knives pushed mercilessly through your back, yet you look your enemies in the face still loving, smiling, and being courteous, as God had commanded you. I am sure that many of us are often tempted to get even, but we should always be mindful that vengeance belongs to God. Our battles are His, and we must learn how to hold our peace even in trying circumstances. God has our backs, and even though the weapons sometimes formed against us, they will not prosper.

I have painfully discovered that when your Chaldeans cannot control you, they will try to destroy you. They will do anything and use anyone in an attempt to bring about your destruction physically, psychologically, financially, socially, spiritually, or by plain character assassination. Their motive is to frustrate your purpose so much that you become disillusioned and lose all hope, joy, and strength to pursue your destiny.

At times like that, we must refocus our thinking and ask why God allows us to experience trials and difficulties. We can find comfort in the fact that our God is still in control of our Chaldeans, our enemies, and their longevity is in His hands.

Your Trials Mature You

Muscles are strengthened and developed through exercise; the more you work them, the better they will function. The more they are stretched, the stronger they become. Believers are assured that their afflictions are good for them because they have a purpose—to transform and transition them to a level in God where their faith is further strengthened and settled.

Your trials are designed to mature and refine you, so do not run away from them or allow yourself to react impulsively before the work that was intended is accomplished. Your trials can bless and reposition you to another level where you will learn to praise God in the midst of your storms and even praise him for the storms themselves! When you look back, you will realize the storms were designed to mature you. You learn to give God thanks in all your circumstances knowing you will come out better if you keep the right attitude.

> Humble yourselves therefore under the mighty hand of God, that he may exalt you in due time: Casting all your care upon him; for he careth for you. Be sober, be vigilant; because your adversary the devil, as a roaring lion, walketh about, seeking whom he may devour: Whom resist stedfast in the faith, knowing that the same afflictions are accomplished in your brethren that are in the world. But the God of all grace, who hath called us unto his eternal glory by Christ Jesus, after that ye have suffered a while, make you perfect, stablish, strengthen, settle you (1 Peter 5:6–10)

Keep Your Dream Alive

Your enemy seeks to distract you from accomplishing your dreams through intimidating and frustrating tactics designed to derail, abort, and delay the fulfillment of your purpose. Your Chaldeans may sell you into slavery as Joseph experienced, but your destiny is assured. They may believe that your future is over, but God allows them to do their thing and shows up to demonstrate that He is God alone.

You exist primarily to fulfill your divine assignment. Trust God to direct, correct, and instruct you on how to fulfill the mandate He has given you. The days of your Chaldeans are numbered, they may get you thrown in the fire, but they do not know your King is waiting there for you. He is invisible until your arrival, and then He will show Himself; even your Nebuchadnezzar will acknowledge that someone is in your fire with you whom he did not put there.

Chaldeans have a mission, and believers should understand that so they can focus on the fulfillment of their assignments. The believers' responses ought to be seasoned with love, compassion, and forgiveness.

> But I say unto you, Love your enemies, bless them that curse you, do good to them that hate you, and pray for

them which despitefully use you, and persecute you; That ye may be the children of your Father which is in heaven: for he maketh his sun to rise on the evil and on the good, and sendeth rain on the just and on the unjust. For if ye love them which love you, what reward have ye? Do not even the publicans the same? And if ye salute your brethren only, what do ye more than others? Do not even the publicans so? (Matthew 5:44–47)

Stick to Your Mission

The believers' mission in life is to please God, no one else. This automatically makes believers targets for the enemy. The enemy wishes to control, manipulate, direct, instruct, and influence their decisions.

Stick to your mission by remaining vigilant and alert to the tactics of the evil one. Do not lose your identity trying to conform to the wishes of people. Do you—be you. You have been designed by God with what you need to fulfill His purpose for your life.

Too many believers are busy doing what they believe should be done but are not doing what they were called to do.

Your Purpose Will Attract Your Enemies

It is amazing how your Chaldeans will swarm around you from all directions as soon as you begin to become what God had destined you to be. They might have been silent and undetectable, but as soon as you stop playing church and began to be the church, your player-haters will come at you just as Goliath did David. Often, you will wonder what you had done that resulted in such heavy attacks particularly at the hands of those you thought were your friends and meant you well.

As I write this chapter, I am under Gulf War–type attacks from many areas. People you really thought meant you well seem to change overnight. They have smiles on their faces but vengeance in their minds and rusty knives in one hand at their backs. I am talking about churchgoing saints who claim to love you and the Lord but are ready to destroy, downplay, frustrate, and abort the prophetic babies you are pregnant with. If you have not seen your enemies emerge, then I challenge you to begin a bible study, a ministry of feeding the poor, loving addicts, and caring for the disadvantaged. I guarantee that you will observe them surfacing with unforgiving vengeance in their eyes holding bloodthirsty spears.

During these times of trials and weighty attacks, you are reminded to allow God to fight for you because your battles are His. Do not use the armor of flesh; do as David did—choose what you know has been tested and anointed for your victory. Use what had kept you safe from the lions, bears, and the Goliaths that come out against your purpose. Pick up your stones of prayer, praise, love, kindness, and forgiveness, then allow God to do the rest. It is not easy to hold your peace in the midst of an unprovoked storm, but the God we serve can give us the strength to endure; we should trust Him to fight our battles.

Encourage Yourself in the Lord—Keep Your Head Up

Your Chaldeans often come out at you with nasty, wicked, and destructive intentions. They seek to destroy your purpose. Do not take their attacks personally; rather, keep your head up and encourage yourself in the Lord. Your King is fighting for you at your side. Relax and remind yourself, *God got this*!

> I will lift up mine eyes unto the hills, from whence cometh my help. My help cometh from the Lord, which made heaven and earth. He will not suffer thy foot to be moved: he that keepeth thee will not slumber. Behold, he that keepeth Israel shall neither slumber nor sleep. The Lord is thy keeper: the Lord is thy shade upon thy right hand. The sun shall not smite thee by day, nor the moon by night. The Lord shall preserve thee from all evil: he shall preserve thy soul. The Lord shall preserve thy going out and thy coming in from this time forth, and even for evermore. (Psalm 121)

I waited patiently for the Lord; and he inclined unto me, and heard my cry. He brought me up also out of an horrible pit, out of the miry clay, and set my feet upon a rock, and established my goings. And he hath put a new song in my mouth, even praise unto our God: many shall see it, and fear, and shall trust in the Lord. (Psalm 40:1–3)

God Will Deliver You

There will be times in your walk with God that the enemy's attacks will be so discouraging that you may feel like giving up. Many times I did not want to see anyone because I wondered if they believed the destructive reports of the enemy. I have asked myself many times, *Whose report will I believe?* I am settled in believing the report of the Lord. Regardless of the impact of the Chaldeans on your life, remember that God has assured you that He is your refuge and will secure your inheritance of the Promised Land.

Mark the perfect man, and behold the upright: for the end of that man is peace. But the transgressors shall be destroyed together: the end of the wicked shall be cut off. But the salvation of the righteous is of the Lord: he is their strength in the time of trouble. And the Lord shall help them, and deliver them: he shall deliver them from the wicked, and save them, because they trust in him. (Psalm 37:37–40)

Allow God to Fight Your Battles

One of the hardest tasks for many believers is to mature to the level that they can relax and allow God to fight their battles. Resisting the temptation to get even with the Chaldeans who seek to destroy believers' characters, purposes, and missions is a sign of spiritual maturity.

God is the defender, the judge, and the jury. Hold your head high and trust God with your situation; He has you covered. Speak to yourself and remind your flesh that God knows whom to fight, how to fight, when to fight, where to fight, and what to use in the fight, so allow Him to fight for you. He has an impressive record; He has never lost a fight. God will deliver and promote you after the fight in the presence of your Chaldeans.

> Yea, though I walk through the valley of the shadow of death, I will fear no evil: for thou art with me; thy rod and thy staff they comfort me. Thou preparest a table before me in the presence of mine enemies: thou anointest my head with oil; my cup runneth over. Surely goodness and mercy shall follow me all the days of my life: and I will dwell in the house of the Lord forever. (Psalm 23:4–6)

God will often orchestrate situations that end up with your enemies seeking your forgiveness. Do not allow bitterness and pride to consume you; demonstrate a Christlike response, forgive, and move on. It was never about you anyway; it was an attack on the baby in you waiting to be born. Your baby is the reason why your player-haters are so consumed by your existence. They talk about you and will organize themselves into attack groups because the devil knows your baby will be a blessings to your generation and those to come.

Pharaoh tried to kill all the Egyptian babies because a baby, a deliverer by the name of Moses, had been born. Herod tried to kill all the babies because a King called Jesus was born. But the God I serve will always preserve His own. He will make a way even if it is in the enemy's own house to secure the destiny of those He has predestined to fulfill His mandate on earth. My God is so awesome! He could allow your enemy to educate you, clothe you, feed you, secure you, socialize you, and still use you to destroy their kingdom.

Yes, people you have been a blessing to are often the very ones trying to destroy you. It will hurt, but forgive them so God can prepare your table in their presence. Do not hinder your blessings by harboring hatred and unforgiveness; your destiny is too great to be delayed. God has a way of allowing your enemies to live long enough to see when and how He blesses you.

Recently, I spoke with a brother in the Lord who had spread some malicious rumors about me that he knew were false and revengeful. I indicated to him that I knew he was the author of such rumors; he did not deny that, but he tried to deflect responsibility for spreading the rumors. I looked him in the eyes and told him I wanted him to know the God I served would have him right there to see when He gets His glory out of that situation. My friend, nearly two years later, that gentleman was sure enough present when God stepped in and shut the lion's mouth, rescued me from the pit of my enemies, and opened up new doors filled with blessings.

God Knows Your Enemies by Name

The enemy tends to operate like an undercover agent. Often, the identity and source of the attack is unknown. This can be confusing when the gossip, lies, and slanderous arrows begin to overwhelm you. During such times, God wants us to be still and let Him be God. People will be people. They may smile with you, assure you that they support you, and tell you what an awesome leader, pastor, executive, or manager you are, yet they simultaneously plot your destruction.

Jesus knows what you are going through. He traveled your journey before and knows your enemies by name. Judas was a part of Jesus's leadership team; he was called out by the Savior around the table to do what he had to do while they ate their last meal together.

Believers ought to mature to the level that they can tell their enemies to do what they planned so God can do what He has to do. Your destiny awaits you, but betrayal, hatred, denial, and loneliness must be conquered.

Many of our Chaldeans do not even know why they are doing what they are doing. This is why their attacks should not be taken personally; our struggles are not with flesh and blood but with satanic forces that can sniff out our destinies and taste our purposes. Do not lose time trying to discover who your haters are and why they hate; focus instead on your destiny. God knows their names; that ought to be enough for you. God will visit them in His time.

Pursue Your Destiny

Trying to detect who your Chaldeans are is a waste of precious time and energy. Use that time to pursue your destiny. Many of them would not admit they hate or envy you, so why bother? Let God deal with them. People can be a distraction from the pursuit of your destiny. God patiently awaits your full attention.

Your Chaldeans will help you develop your spiritual stamina and character. Let your transformation process refine and prepare you to appreciate, respect, and accept the new blessings in your new levels after your storm. The storm you are going through has been divinely designed to sharpen your character and strengthen your faith.

Do not touch your enemy; be still and allow your process to be complete. They can help push you into your destiny. David had many opportunities to destroy King Saul, but he refused because he knew his destiny was too important to waste it seeking revenge. David told Saul, "May the Lord avenge the wrongs you have done to me, but my hands will not touch you" (1 Samuel 24:12). Like David, I too have had many tempting opportunities to destroy the careers of those who had done me wrong, but it is always better to stay out of God's business.

God is waiting for our characters to mature before He brings us out. He always has a greater plan for us. This book is a product of the valuable lessons I have learned during my troubles and battles. God in His wisdom permitted the Chaldeans to attack me so He could birth this book out of me. It was in my belly for several months being matured by my trouble, trials, tribulations, and frustrations.

The pain of deceit, betrayal, and gossip have strengthened me and allowed me to push this baby out. Look at what the Lord had done! Your mess can be transformed into a message, your stress into a blessing, your obstacles into opportunities, your hatred into love, your bad days into good days, and your weeping into laughter. Your weeping may be for a while, but joy is coming in your morning.

Too Blessed to Be Stressed

When you comprehend the calling on your life, you will not allow the trials to stress you out; you will appreciate why you are going through them. Your purpose is too great to squander your energy, time, and resources fighting in the flesh. Your weapons as a believer are not carnal but supernatural. Seek God's direction about how to respond to your Chaldeans. The call on your life demands a mature Christian response.

Focus on where God is taking you rather than on the storms you are going through. People will often look at you and see what they could have become but did not have the courage to go through what you have been through to get where you are today. Friend, someone said it well: "No pain, no gain." I have painfully discovered that those who are bitter and envious of the successes of others are likely candidates to be used by the devil. It does not take much work to fan the fire of hatred, envy, and jealousy; all the devil needs is availability.

How to Manage the Attacks of the Enemy

David understood very well how to manage the attacks of the enemy. He had to hide for several years from King Saul, who was determined to end his life. In Psalm 37, David very methodically expressed ways to respond to the enemy's attacks.

- God will cut your enemies down (vv. 1–2).
- Do not focus on your enemies; rather, delight in the Lord (vv. 3–4).
- Spend your time on your purpose, and God will make you shine (vv. 5–6).
- Take a rest from your enemies, and wait for God to show up (v. 7).
- Refuse to allow anger to control your decisions (v. 8).
- Stop fretting; that just makes your situation worse (v. 8).
- Your blessings will come if you are patient and wait on God (vv. 9–11).
- God can turn things around, and the weapons meant to harm you will harm your enemies (vv. 12–15).
- God will destroy your enemies for you and cause them to perish; He supports the righteous (vv. 17–20).
- Whom God blesses is well blessed (v. 22).
- The steps of a believer are prearranged by God (v. 23).
- Your enemy cannot destroy you when you trust God (v. 24).
- God is your provider, so do not compromise your faith (v. 25).

- The Lord will protect and preserve His own (v. 28).
- Wicked people will always try to destroy you, but the Lord will be your protection (vv. 32–33).
- Wait on God; He will exalt you (vv. 34–36).
- God will be your strength in times of trouble (v. 39).
- The Lord Himself will deliver you (v. 40).

Trust God, and Do Not Be Afraid

The God who had promoted and blessed you is able to keep you covered from the arrows of the wicked one. Your Chaldeans have a set time and season to trouble you, and when that time is over, it's over. There is no need to fear; you are assured that God specializes in hiding you in His tabernacle. You can have peace in the midst of your storms because God is your protector; you have no need to fear. When false witnesses rise up against you, the Lord will step in and cover you from their arrows and wicked devices. There is no need to be fearful because God will illuminate your path and give you the strength for the battle you are in. David knew how to trust God and not be afraid.

Psalm 27 has been a comfort for me during my troubles. I have learned what it meant to wait on God and watch Him fight on my behalf. Your Chaldeans are always seeking for ways to ensnare, trip up, or derail you from your destiny. I have painfully experienced how false witnesses can rise up against you and exhale their envy, lies, and innuendos. But for God, I would have been destroyed and consumed.

A Letter to My Adversaries

Dear Friends,

I am thankful for the humbling experience and say a resounding thank you to all of you who spoke the truth, lied, gossiped, despised, laughed, plotted, orchestrated, and desired my demise.

Please know that you have helped me mature, refocus, and realign my priorities on the things that matter, the pursuit of God's purpose for my life. You have pushed me into deeper spiritual growth, and I am a better man because of you. The lessons learned have been imbedded on the table of my heart. Subsequently, I am repositioning my life to receive the blessings of God.

Just like Joseph, what you meant to destroy me and my family has been turned around by God to bless and lift us higher. Thank you for the pit, for without it, we could not get to the palace. We now understand that God was behind it all the time, and it was good that we have been afflicted. Through our affliction, we patiently learned how to use God's Word, pray for results, fast effectively, trust God, and allow Him to fight for us. Your setups and setbacks were just preparation for our comeback.

My family and I are praying for you, and we love you because God has used you to transition us higher. Your season is ended, and as we transition higher, we know we will have new devils at our new levels. In spite of that, we count it all joy. To God be the glory for the great things He has done!

In Christ,
Mr. Cleveland Ramsey

Count It All Joy

Do not fear the false witnesses who have joined forces to attack your credibility and purpose. Trust God; rely on Him to vindicate you. God will not allow anything to happen to you without His permission. Is it not ironic that people who could not tolerate each other can miraculously join forces together to attack you? There is no need to fear when you know in whom you have placed your trust.

God will bring you out of the traps and snares of your enemies. He specializes in converting the bad that was perpetuated against you into a blessing for you. Believers ought to get to the point in their lives that they begin a celebration of praise to God for His divine protection, when they consider the evil agenda of their enemies. We have been advised to count it all joy knowing good will come out of our trials when we possess the righteous attitude during our tests and trials (James 1:2–4).

Joseph's brothers thought that they had silenced his dream; they did not know God was orchestrating a more profound plan to push Joseph toward his destiny and the fulfillment of his purpose. God was preparing Joseph for leadership so he could rescue the very brothers who had sold him into slavery. What an amazing God we serve!

It is comforting to know your enemies cannot stop, delay, abort, or deny the purpose of God for your life. When they seek to destroy you, God will use their lies and hatred to reposition you toward your destiny. I am a living Joseph who continues to trust in the awesome power of God to deliver me from the wicked snares and plots of my enemies.

As you get closer to your destiny, be assured that the fire and darts from your enemies will become more intense. The intensity of their attacks is an indication you are purposed for greatness. The greatness you are pregnant with has attracted the attention of your enemy, who gets stronger, more ferocious, craftier, and strategic.

Prepare for New Devils at Your New Levels

As God transitions you and shifts you in His divine plan for your life, realize you will experience new devils at your new levels. God is up to something when your troubles seem to double and your tests seem unbearable. Trust God; allow His power to see you through. You need faith to endure times like those. Prepare to be talked about, lied about, persecuted, and isolated as you experience new levels of blessings. You see, the enemy assumes you will give up and give in if the heat is turned up against you. He hopes you will abort your baby before it comes to maturity.

Position yourself through consistent prayers, fasting, and the study of God's Word so you will be fortified when the attacks come. The enemy is hoping you will be too distracted and discouraged to appreciate the many blessings and favors you will receive at your new level in God. If you are not prayerful, pride and arrogance can subtly creep into your heart until you begin to praise yourself for the accomplishments attained and the dangerous battles won.

Your enemies cannot stand to see you prospering in the midst of your storms. Your storms will not kill you; they will be your taxi ride to your next level in God. Yes, you will observe that some people you once considered friends, coworkers, and associates will begin to act in very crazy ways as if you were never known. Strangely enough, many whom you once considered friends will show their envy and jealousy when they see you can still function with a smile in the middle of your storm.

Your Chaldeans will push you into a fire, but God has sanctioned that fire to purify you for the next level of blessings. Your promotion is after the fire. Do not fear the fire; your God is waiting to cover you with His arms from the heat intended to consume you.

Your next level will expose and awaken new devils. As you transition to your next level of faith, God will be with you. You may not see Him, but if you trust Him with your life as the three Hebrew boys did, He will reveal Himself, and your enemies will see Him protecting you in your fire. Your enemies will have to call you out of what they put you in. That is why I am learning each day to say, "Thanks for the fire!"

Key Points to Remember

- ✓ Your new levels will definitely attract new devils.
- ✓ Your player-haters have a purpose; they will help you develop spiritual stamina.
- ✓ Take comfort in the fact that your enemies cannot stop, delay, abort, or deny the purpose of God for your life.
- ✓ Your trials are designed with your maturity in mind.
- ✓ Your purpose attracts your enemies.
- ✓ Your enemy seeks to distract you from accomplishing your dreams through intimidating and frustrating tactics designed to derail, abort, and delay the fulfillment of your purpose.
- ✓ Hold your head up and learn to encourage yourself in the Lord.

✓ Keep your composure, and allow God to fight your battles for you His way.

✓ God knows your enemies by name, so focus on pursuing your destiny.

✓ Learn how to manage the attacks of the enemies rather than allowing them to stress you out.

✓ Position yourself through consistent prayers, fasting, and the study of God's Word so you will be fortified when the attacks come.

✓ The enemy is hoping you will be distracted and discouraged so much that you do not appreciate the many new blessings and favor of your new levels in God.

✓ Your enemies cannot stand to see you prospering in the midst of your storms.

✓ Your storms will not kill you; they will be your taxi ride to your next level in God.

✓ Trust God, and do not fear your enemies.

✓ God will bring you out of the traps and snares of your enemies.

✓ Count it all joy!

CHAPTER 5

TRANSFORMATION IN THE FIRE—
THANKS FOR THE FIRE!

Gold cannot be processed in the absence of intense heat, which purifies it. The fire serves as a sterilizer, disinfectant, decontaminator, and separator for the extraction of the authentic gold.

The fire the believer encounters has a divine assignment to kill and purify the flesh and purge that believer of worldly imperfections and contaminants. Our vessels need spiritual detoxification of all the pollutants that have gravitated to attack the purposes of God. The frequent fire that believers experience will do that and position them for greatness.

Scripture reminds us that our attitude should be appreciative and that we ought to look to God each day and declare, "Thanks for the fire!"

> James, a servant of God and of the Lord Jesus Christ, to the twelve tribes which are scattered abroad, greeting. My brethren, count it all joy when ye fall into divers temptations; Knowing this, that the trying of your faith worketh patience. But let patience have her perfect work, that ye may be perfect and entire, wanting nothing. If any of you lack wisdom, let him ask of God, that giveth to all men liberally, and upbraideth not; and it shall be given him. But let him ask in faith, nothing wavering. For he that wavereth is like a wave of the sea driven with the wind and tossed. (James 1:1–6)

And I will bring the third part through the fire, and will refine them as silver is refined, and will try them as gold is tried: they shall call on my name, and I will hear them: I will say, It is my people: and they shall say, The Lord is my God. (Zechariah 13:9)

But now thus saith the Lord that created thee, O Jacob, and he that formed thee, O Israel, Fear not: for I have redeemed thee, I have called thee by thy name; thou art mine. When thou passest through the waters, I will be with thee; and through the rivers, they shall not overflow thee: when thou walkest through the fire, thou shalt not be burned; neither shall the flame kindle upon thee. (Isaiah 43:1–2)

Do Not Panic—Your Fire Is only a Test

God knows what is best for His children. God has a purpose for every trial we go through, and no one can stop, delay, or deny His purposes for His children. He has a unique way of allowing uncomfortable circumstances into the lives of believers He has designed to strengthen their characters.

The fires, troubles, or trials in your life are often direct signals that God is preparing and positioning you for your next level of blessings. The fires authenticate the believers' salvation. However, having a relationship with God does not exempt you from going through the fire. Frequently, some believers find themselves caught up in pity parties complaining about how hot and unpleasant the fires in their lives are. However, I believe God wants you to focus on what He is taking you to rather than on what you are going through!

Your fire is intended to get you to your blessings that are on the other side of your fire. God is expecting you to show up, grow up, and refuse to give up. The Chaldeans or enemies in your life always look for opportunities to gossip about you to the king according to Daniel 3:1–16. They are motivated by envy, jealousy, and pride, and they hope to get that little bit of information on you that they think will be your downfall. But when God is with you, you have no need to fear; you can speak truth to power without fear or contradiction. There is no need to panic; it is only a test.

> Shadrach, Meshach, and Abednego, answered and said to the king, O Nebuchadnezzar, we are not careful to answer thee in this matter. If it be so, our God whom we serve is able to deliver us from the burning fiery furnace, and he will deliver us out of thine hand, O king. But if not, be it known unto thee, O king that we will not serve thy gods, nor worship the golden image which thou hast set up. Then was Nebuchadnezzar full of fury, and the form of his visage was changed against Shadrach, Meshach, and Abednego: therefore he spake, and commanded that they should heat the furnace one seven times more than it was wont to be heated. And he commanded the most mighty men that were in his army to bind Shadrach, Meshach, and Abednego, and to cast them into the burning fiery furnace. Then these men were bound in their coats, their hosen, and their hats, and their other garments, and were cast into the midst of the burning fiery furnace. (Daniel 3:16–21)

Do Not Despise Your Fire—God Wants to Get His Glory Out of It

Our blessings as Christians are often mysteriously packaged in trials, storms, or life-threatening difficulties meant to push us and challenge our faith in God. During those times, we may be tempted to despise a situation God has divinely ordained and appointed to bring about His blessings. Sometimes, God allows circumstances in the lives of His children so truth can be told to power, but too often, we give up, give in, and become intimidated because the fire around us has been turned up seven times hotter.

The fire you are experiencing as a Christian has a purpose attached to it—to transform you so you can become better rather than bitter. God does not make mistakes; He knows what you need for your blessings to be manifested.

The three Hebrew boys did not despise the fire God had allowed to come their way. What seems like trouble is usually God's way of transitioning us to another level. As Christians, we are to trust God with the process because He knows what He is doing. Though the journey may be painful and life threatening, we are called upon to rely on God to take us through our difficulties.

> Thou broughtest us into the net; thou laidst affliction upon our loins. Thou hast caused men to ride over our heads; we went through fire and through water: but thou broughtest us out into a wealthy place. (Psalm 66:11–12)

> Cast thy burden upon the Lord, and he shall sustain thee: he shall never suffer the righteous to be moved. But thou, O God, shalt bring them down into the pit of destruction: bloody and deceitful men shall not live out half their days; but I will trust in thee. (Psalm 55:22–23)

Christians ought to remind themselves nothing can impact them unless God has given His endorsement. The fire is sent to bless, correct, direct, instruct, or lead believers to righteous streams. If God allows the trouble to be brought to you, He will take you through it into a more productive and prosperous place.

Stand for Righteousness and Speak Truth to Power Notwithstanding the Enemy's Threats

The three Hebrew boys were unified in their righteous position. They spoke with one voice to the king and without fear declared they would not eat his food, worship his idol, or dance to his music. Believers ought to observe the action of these three boys who did not change their minds because they were facing possible death. God honors commitment and dedication to His Word. They did not blame anyone or try to deflect their punishment; they made their position clear and stood by their word.

God looks for believers who stand for holiness in spite of imminent danger. Christians are to be courageous and make their righteous positions known to the kings of our day.

Do Not Fear Your Fire

The three Hebrew boys were not intimidated by the fire. The enemy will do all he can to plant fear in believers' hearts to dampen their faith. The Christian's hope and trust is in God, who promises to be with His children always.

> Fear thou not; for I am with thee: be not dismayed; for I am thy God: I will strengthen thee; yea, I will help thee; yea, I will uphold thee with the right hand of my righteousness. (Isaiah 41:10)

> Be strong and of a good courage, fear not, nor be afraid of them: for the Lord thy God, he it is that doth go with thee; he will not fail thee, nor forsake thee. (Deuteronomy 31:6)

> God is our refuge and strength, a very present help in trouble. Therefore will not we fear, though the earth be removed, and though the mountains be carried into the midst of the sea. (Psalm 46:1–2)

Do Not Compromise Your Integrity to Get along with Any Worldly King

Too often, many Christians back up and give in because the fire or trouble is turned up by the enemy; they compromise their standards to accommodate the kings of this world. This is regularly done through attempts to dilute the potency of the Word of God so it would be more digestible and acceptable to the powerful forces of this world. The three boys did not compromise their righteous integrity to accommodate their enemy. Every believer should learn from their behavior.

- **The three Hebrew boys' faith in God was strengthened.** Trouble sent to destroy you can strengthen your faith in God. Your fiery trials should be celebrated; they are signs God is in control. According to Isiah 54:17, we are assured that weapons will be formed but will not prosper.
- **They were prepared to die for what they believed in.** The enemy will test your faith to see if you are prepared to die for what you believe in. Christians' lives ought to be hidden in Christ.
- **They accepted their fire like soldiers in the army of God.** The young men told their enemy that they were prepared to die rather than eat his food, dance to his music, or worship his gods. We ought to be just as resilient in our faith by standing up for our beliefs even in the face of danger.
- **They maintained a righteous attitude in spite of their fire.** The boys held their attitude to the highest standard in spite of the trouble they were experiencing. They made their position known to the king in a very respectful manner. They did not use profanity or call their accusers by derogatory names. Their faith in God was enough to make their position clearly known without fear of the hungry fire that was their intended end.

    Too often, many believers display a faulty reflection of our Lord and Savior Jesus Christ when they seek to fight fire with fire. The battle of the Christian belongs to God because He will fight for them. Hold your head high; allow God to be glorified.
- **They gave themselves to God so He could use them.** They acknowledged that their lives were not theirs; they released them to God so He could do with them what He desired even if it meant their death. God wants His children to trust Him completely with their lives.

Back Up, Devil!

The fire killed those who had thrown the three Hebrew boys into the fire. Back up, devil! You have gone as far as you were supposed to. The bad being done to you has an end. Your enemies cannot exceed the boundaries God has set for them. God will allow the fire meant for you to be turned on your haters.

> And he commanded the most mighty men that were in his army to bind Shadrach, Meshach, and Abednego, and to cast them into the burning fiery furnace. Then these men were bound in their coats, their hosen, and their hats, and their other garments, and were cast into the midst of the burning fiery furnace. Therefore because the king's commandment was urgent, and the furnace exceeding hot, the flames of the fire slew those men that took up Shadrach, Meshach, and Abednego. (Daniel 3:20–24)

When God is in your fire, He will handle your enemies for you. By protecting the Hebrew boys, God was saying, "Devil, stop there! My boys have demonstrated their commitment, and you have done what you were allowed to do. I'll take over from here. These are my children, and all now know their faith is anchored in me. There is nothing you could have done, devil, to keep them away from praising me. You lost. Take your hand off my children now they are in my care!"

When your enemies turn up the heat seven times hotter with the intention of destroying you, just let them try. Ironically, they do not know the number seven is a significant number that will work to your advantage. God rested on the seventh day, and He will give you rest too from all your player-haters who have been gossiping, lying, plotting, and waiting to see you burn in their fire.

God watches over His own; He knows their struggles, pains, and frustrations. When His children cry out to Him, He comes to their rescue; He takes care of those who try to demand that His children worship their gods.

The enemy may tie us up and throw us in flaming situations that they think will consume and destroy us, but our God has a greater plan and is patiently waiting in our fire for us.

It is perfectly fine if my enemies bring me to my knees. They do not understand they are doing me a favor because that position is God's position. They threw the boys in, and they fell down because they were bound (Daniel 3:23). My friend, our God will show up and reveal Himself for all to see when we get in position on our knees.

God Is Waiting for You in Your Fire

> And these three men, Shadrach, Meshach, and Abednego, fell down bound into the midst of the burning fiery furnace. Then Nebuchadnezzar the king was astonished, and rose up in haste, and spake, and said unto his counsellors, Did not we cast three men bound into the midst of the fire? They answered and said unto the king, True, O king. He answered and said, Lo, I see four men loose, walking in the midst of the fire, and they have no hurt; and the form of the fourth is like the Son of God. (Daniel 3:23–25)

The Son of God was waiting in their fire, and their enemies recognized Him. When we fall, God is in our fiery situations and will pick us up. When we fall, our God will reveal Himself and show up. God will show up in our marriages, jobs, finances—every area of our lives—when we get on our knees in His presence.

Friend, your enemies would not believe their eyes when they see God with you in your fire. Trusting God completely will guarantee His protection and presence right in the midst of your fire. Your haters will see you raise your hands released from bondage and held high in reverence to give God the praise. Your mouth will be released to sing songs of praise, and your unshackled feet will dance in worship before your God.

Whatever the enemy uses to intimidate you will be what God reveals Himself in. God has promised us He will do the following and much more.

- Lift up all His children who fall and those who are bowed down.
- Bring meat in due season to those who wait on Him.
- Be with us because He has chosen us and will not throw us away.
- Strengthen us and help us.

- Make our enemies ashamed and bewildered.
- Make as nothing those who fight us.

> Thy kingdom is an everlasting kingdom, and thy dominion endureth throughout all generations. The Lord upholdeth all that fall, and raiseth up all those that be bowed down. The eyes of all wait upon thee; and thou givest them their meat in due season. (Psalm 145:13–15)

> Thou whom I have taken from the ends of the earth, and called thee from the chief men thereof, and said unto thee, Thou art my servant; I have chosen thee, and not cast thee away. Fear thou not; for I am with thee: be not dismayed; for I am thy God: I will strengthen thee; yea, I will help thee; yea, I will uphold thee with the right hand of my righteousness. Behold, all they that were incensed against thee shall be ashamed and confounded: they shall be as nothing; and they that strive with thee shall perish. (Isaiah 41:9–11)

Freed by Fire

The three boys were loosed in the fire. Their enemy saw that his fire freed them from their bonds. Your fire has a purpose. God wants to break the chains that others have imposed on you—chains of oppression, depression, lack, tradition, strongholds, and generational curses. All can be broken by the fire because God is with you. Where the Spirit of the Lord is, there will be liberty. God has orchestrated some fire in our lives to set us free to praise Him. When He is in your fire, the fire meant to harm you will release you according to Daniel 3:25: "I see four men loose, walking in the midst of the fire."

God will sometimes use your fire to get the attention of the enemy. Your enemy will see his efforts to kill and immobilize you cannot work. When God prepares your table even in the midst of your fire, your enemy will be there to see. The trouble or fire the enemy sent to destroy you will burn your bonds. Your worship in your fire will shift whatever atmosphere you find yourself in. You have been set free to give God the glory.

Maturity in Your Fire

You can be freed from every bond your enemy has restrained you with. You have the power to walk and function in whatever the enemy sends your way. The boys were walking in the fire intended to kill them. Can you stand up in what was meant to kill you? Yes, you can as long as God is with you. He promised He will be with you.

Walk in your fire. Let it mature you. Function right in what was intended to afflict you with hurt, pain, destruction, and death. God is with you to enable you to live in the fire that ought to kill you. Walk and give God the glory for protecting you from the consuming flames waiting to devour you if God had not been at your side. Walk through what was sent to destroy you. Let your enemies see that your trouble is not about them, but so that God with you in the fire could be glorified!

> He restoreth my soul: he leadeth me in the paths of righteousness for his name's sake. Yea, though I walk through the valley of the shadow of death, I will fear no evil: for thou art with me; thy rod and thy staff they comfort me. Thou preparest a table before me in the presence of mine enemies: thou anointest my head with oil; my cup runneth over. (Psalm 23:3–5)

Your enemy will see your God and know He is greater. The three boys' enemy saw that his fire was not consuming the boys. Your haters will be amazed to see that their traps, plots, and heat cannot harm you. Take authority over your circumstances, and show the enemy your God will protect you from any fire. Your battle belongs to God.

The lost world needs to see us as believers walking in our fires. Our marriages, children, jobs, spouses, businesses, governments, and churches need us to keep on walking.

Friend, God has spoken concerning your situation, and all we have to do is say amen and keep on walking.

- Walking in your fire is telling the enemy you are alive and well.
- Walking in your fire symbolizes apostolic authority over your situation.
- Walking in your fire tells the enemy his plans and plots for your demise have been canceled.
- Walking in your fire is a testimony to the greatness of your God.
- Walking in your fire shows functionality and progression.
- Walking in your fire shows you are a vessel of faith who depends on God.

Your walking in your fire will blow your enemy's mind; he will have to submit to the God you serve and acknowledge He is greater than him and ought to be praised. The enemy had to call the boys out of what he put them in; your enemy will have to do the same. He will have to reverse his plans concerning you and acknowledge the greatness of your God.

You Will Not Look or Smell Like What You Have Been Through

First, your enemies will meticulously observe that you do not smell like the smoke and fire you have been experiencing. Second, they will see you do not look like what you have gone through. Third, they will see what they put you through did not affect you. The fire of your enemies will not harm you the way they intended when God is in your fire with you. Your enemies will see Him protecting you.

The illness that had you hospitalized and near death will be done away with, and you will not look like where you have been because your King will have visited your bedside during your medical fire. The court case that could have incarcerated you and left your haters smiling will be interrupted by your Advocate, who will adjudicate your case, and declare you free from the envious chains that had kept you bound. Your smile, health, and peace of mind will return to you.

Your Fire Is Not Always about You

The fire you are going through has a divine assignment that may involve many other people; check your attitude in the midst of the wrongdoing you are suffering. It is instinctive to want to fight fire with fire and seek revenge when you are being punished by your enemies because of your refusal to dance to their music, eat their food, and worship their earthly, materialistic gods.

> But as for you, ye thought evil against me; but God meant it unto good, to bring to pass, as it is this day, to save much people alive. (Genesis 50:20)

> For I know the thoughts that I think toward you, saith the Lord, thoughts of peace, and not of evil, to give you an expected end. (Jeremiah 29:11)

Believers' troubles are not always just about them. Believers can easily develop selfish and arrogant perspectives thinking their struggles are all about them. God's plan is bigger than ours, and He wants our testimonies to be so anointed that they impact nations and generations to come. The world is attentively watching to see the Christlike attitude we display during our trials. As ambassadors of the kingdom, our reactions to our persecutors should always be seasoned with forgiveness and love.

Your Promotion Comes after Your Fire

The enemy had to bless the boys by promoting them after the fire. Nebuchadnezzar accepted the boys' God as greater and more powerful than his. The first thing he did was to change the policy to favor the three Hebrew boys. He instructed all to worship their God or face severe punishment. Second, he promoted the boys right over the very Chaldeans who had gossiped about the boys and who wanted them to die.

God will promote you right over your haters who have gossiped about you to the authorities on your job, community, or country. God will deal with your enemies in His time and in His way. He will have every one of them present to observe when He blesses you, turns your situation around, and prepares your table of blessings in their faces.

Thanks for the Fire!

Joseph looked back over His life and did not hate his brothers for all the wrongs they had done to him. He concluded that God had enabled him to position himself to bless those who had hated him according to Genesis 50:15–21. Joseph understood that his promotion was through the fire, so he humbled himself and stayed prayerful throughout all the injustices done to him.

The Hebrew boys' fire was intended to bless them. Do not allow the heat of the fire to frighten or intimidate you and cause you to abort prematurely your process. Those boys would not have experienced their blessings had they given in to the fire. I have lived long enough and have gone through enough to understand that our problems are often the divine vehicle by which God elevates us.

The wrongs perpetuated against you are working for you. We Christians are often perplexed and distressed by the many storms, trials, and fires we encounter daily, but God wants us to understand that our trials are preparing and positioning us for the next level of blessings, a new season in our lives. How we master our present will determine how we respond to our tomorrow.

The Hebrew boys substantiated that obedience to God even when threatened by death was right and would bring blessings. Refusal to submit to a Nebuchadnezzar is honored by God and is a great authentication of His awesome power. Be encouraged; you may weep now, but your joy is coming in your morning. Your Good Friday may be excruciating and despondent, but hold your head high because your Sunday morning will soon come.

Your promotion will come right after the fire, so thank God for all He has brought you through, all the hills He gave you the strength to climb, the obstacles to overcome, and the wisdom to escape the many snares of the enemy. Your fire can get you to your blessings, so do not leave your furnace until God shows up to bless you.

Comrades, raise your hands, open your mouths, and give God thanks for the fire that will transition us into our blessings. God wants us to be brave knowing He will be with us and carry us through all the fire and storms in our lives. God is constantly assuring us each day that He is the ultimate Judge who will overrule any fiery situation, your haters, or your hungry lions sent by the enemy to attack you.

Key Points to Remember

- ✓ The fire that the believer encounters has a divine assignment to kill and purify the flesh and purge that believer of worldly imperfections and contaminants.
- ✓ Do not panic; your fire is only a test.
- ✓ Do not despise your fire because God wants to get His glory out of it.
- ✓ Stand for righteousness and speak truth to power notwithstanding the threats of the enemy.
- ✓ Do not compromise your integrity to get along with any king but God.
- ✓ What is happening to you is not always for you or about you.
- ✓ Your haters will be amazed to see that their traps, plots, and heat could not harm you.
- ✓ You have the power to walk and function in whatever the enemy sends your way.
- ✓ Your worship in your fire can shift whatever atmosphere you find yourself in.
- ✓ Do not allow the heat of the fire to frighten or intimidate you and cause you to abort prematurely your process.
- ✓ Your enemy will see your God and know He is greater.
- ✓ The wrongs perpetuated on you will work for you.
- ✓ Your fire can get you to your blessings, so do not leave your furnace until God shows up to bless you.
- ✓ Your promotion is through the fire.

- ✓ Your promotion will come right after the fire, so thank God for all He has brought you through.
- ✓ God will promote you right over your haters who have spoken and gossiped about you to the powers that be on your job or in your community or country.
- ✓ Do not forget to tell your enemies, "Thanks for the fire!"

CHAPTER 6

TRANSFORMATION IN THE MIDST OF ACCUSATION— WHEN GOD OVERRULES

Have you ever been in a situation where you saw no way out of, but God stepped in miraculously and snatched you out of the lion's den just in time? Yes, your enemy may have already planned your economic, social, and religious funerals and have selected your tomb. They may have printed your obituary, cooked the food for the party, killed your reputation by dragging you through the mud, and discussed who would take your position, title, and money, but God stepped in, overruled them, declared you were still His child, interrupted your funeral, and prepared a table of blessings for you in the presence of your enemies!

Others may have given up on you, declared you were finished, and said your future was over. Some may have said that you could never recover from that situation and that your purpose had been aborted, delayed, or even denied. I am thankfully aware that God has the final say concerning your future and that it is not over until He says so. When God says yes, no one can say no, and whom He keeps is well kept. Your lions may roar at you, but they cannot touch you!

Your Lions Cannot Harm You

Daniel was barbarically and maliciously treated then thrown into a den of hungry, ferocious, and unforgiving lions. This happened because he bravely took a religious stand and refused to obey the orders of man to stop praying to his God. Daniel knew the consequences, but he was determined to die if necessary for the God he served and loved dearly.

Daniel's courageousness is a poignant example of what God expects us to do when faced with challenges to our relationship with Him. God showed up in the den of lions, erased their appetites, locked their jaws, and kept Daniel untouched. All night, the lions walked around him and looked at him but could not comprehend why they could not touch him. God had overruled their natural instincts; they had to submit to His divine plan and purpose for Daniel's life.

Early the next day, God allowed the king to check on Daniel and liberate him. God will rule on our behalf and summons those who put us in our situations to pull us out of them. He will shatter the plans of our enemies, frustrate their agenda, and deliver His people on time.

Your Enemies' Days Are Numbered

God numbers the days of your enemies, and when He steps in, they will not be able to execute their malicious, wicked, and hypocritical plans. Your enemies may have smiled and thought they had you where they wanted you for many years. I have come to the sobering realization that the attacks I am undergoing were planned many years ago by those who waited patiently for the right moment to implement their wicked agenda.

When you are most vulnerable, your enemies will attack you and think they have the final say. Friend, the God we serve is still in control of our destinies, and if you adopt the attitude of Daniel, He will fight for you.

When God overrules, He fights for you and does it in style, royally, and prominently so all will realize you serve an awesome God. God wants to get His glory out of your situation. This means that He waits patiently until your enemies are all present before He reveals that table decorated with blessings right in their presence.

> The LORD is my shepherd; I shall not want. He maketh me to lie down in green pastures: he leadeth me beside the still waters. He restoreth my soul: he leadeth me in the paths of righteousness for his name's sake. Yea, though

I walk through the valley of the shadow of death, I will fear no evil: for thou art with me; thy rod and thy staff they comfort me. Thou preparest a table before me in the presence of mine enemies: thou anointest my head with oil; my cup runneth over. Surely goodness and mercy shall follow me all the days of my life: and I will dwell in the house of the LORD forever. (Psalm 23)

God Overrules Your Player-Haters

God overruled on Daniel's behalf, and He did so as well with the woman caught in adultery. Her accusers claimed that the woman found was committing a sin that could be committed only with two characters, yet only one had judgement imposed. Her accusers had already concluded she was the only one at fault because no detail or explanation was offered as to why her accomplice in that crime was blatantly absent. That case from the outset was biased; judgmental fingers pointed at that woman as the only guilty one in that matter. The woman was convicted from the start and was brought to Jesus only to see if perhaps He would uphold their crooked and unjust verdict.

I am amazed of the audacity and nerve of the accusers who thought it necessary to quote scriptures to Jesus to justify their reasoning and behavior toward that woman. They were obviously content that their conclusions were scripturally justifiable according to the laws Moses had given to their forefathers. They were quick to quote the scriptures to judge others' situations, but they themselves were secretly pregnant with iniquities of their own. Perhaps they thought their sins were fine since they were not exposed as that lonely woman had been.

Jesus was concerned about their hypocrisy; the woman's accusers wanted to kill her for a sin because it was publicly known in spite of the fact they had committed similar sins but in private. Jesus saw their inner hearts and hidden faults and knew they should not cast stones. Just as the lions were waiting to tear Daniel apart, so were the woman's accusers who had bloodthirsty lips, unrepentant hearts, revengeful hands, judgmental minds, and university-level hypocrisy.

Jesus in His wisdom saw stones of hatred, unforgiveness, religiosity, pride, arrogance, and hypocrisy. He challenged them to begin the execution if they were without sin. That, my friend, leveled the playing field; many there thought the woman's sin demanded death while taking very little consideration of their own shortcomings.

The Transforming Power of Love

The love Jesus showed for that woman demonstrates to all believers the attitude they should strive for notwithstanding what they think, feel, perceive, or desire to be the outcome of a situation. The attitude of believers ought to be seasoned with love so forgiveness can be easily attained. Love looks beyond the sin and sees the need for deliverance, forgiveness, restoration, and healing. Love looks beyond the sin and the situation of the sinner. I am elated that Jesus's love snatched me from the claws of sin.

Jesus's actions toward that woman reminded her accusers that He was the ultimate judge and they were in no position to cast judgment on her since they too were guilty of sin. Love inspires forgiveness, and when it is demonstrated tangibly, others can experience the power of Calvary, where our Savior died.

Love purges the heart of hatred, bitterness, anger, stress, frustration, depression, unforgiveness, self-righteousness, and hypocrisy. It lowers blood pressure, calms nerves, and flushes out all obstacles in our blood vessels so the blood shed on Calvary can run unabated through our veins. The blood of Jesus is saturated with love and compassion. It has the power to change hearts, transform lives, restore relationships, and mend brokenness. It is not prejudicial, political, selective, or discriminating. It flows to the deepest ocean and climbs the highest mountain searching for broken souls.

Friend, when God overrules, He does so in love. God is concerned more about your future than your past in spite of your shortcomings. God's blood brightens your future and gives you strength to overcome obstacles.

When God Turns Your Pressure into Praise

How God does what He does transforms our thinking about who He is. God often uses our adversities to promote us to a higher level. What often can seem to be trouble, disappointment, frustration, and failure is usually our transformative incubators for the blessings to come.

The pressure from the storms and trials can easily leave you weak and defenseless, but God in His wisdom converts that pressure into praise. The pain and frustration can turn you into a more mature person who will exit the storm stronger, wiser, and more fortified than when you went in.

I am patiently learning not to complain during my storms. Since God was with me when I went in, He will be with me there and bring me out. Our storms often soak us with opportunities for growth financially, spiritually, and psychologically.

God has a plan to bring you out of all situations He has allowed to affect you. The storms of life are subject to His commands and must subside at His request. Your waves may be ferocious, but they will be stilled at God's command; He can bring peace to your storm.

How God Overruled on My Behalf

I had an experience of how God can transform our thinking processes right in the midst of accusation. The world is inundated with envious, jealous, and cold-hearted people who go to unimaginable lengths to distort, destroy, and assassinate the characters and reputations of men and women of God. When others attempt to control, manipulate us, and have limited success, quite often, they seek ways to malign our characters and good names. They will meet, recruit, strategize, and then very meticulously execute their wicked plans designed to cast aspersions and minimize our influence. Nevertheless, that devil and his cohorts are still liars. They will not succeed in their quest to delay the purposes of God

One thing that amazed me during my trials was the fact that my enemies who could not even stand each other joined forces in an attempt to organize my character assassination. Your enemies know how to pull together to attack you, but sad to say, many in the body of Christ have not mastered the concept of being our brothers' and sisters' keepers. I have painfully observed how supposedly saints backed away and played busy when I needed the prayers of those I loved.

God revealed to me that the dark places of my life were fruitful places because like a seed, germination could not occur unless I was covered and buried. My Good Fridays had to be experienced before my Sunday mornings came. I had to go through midnight before daylight came. I began to understand that the dirt thrown on me was to be used as fertilizer for my seed to sprout. This revelation transformed my pressure into praise, my sorrow into laughter, and my pain into gain.

I have been the recipient of encouragement and love from those in the civic and secular areas much more than from my brothers and sisters in the Lord. It seems that many who frequent churches have lost their compassion and love and are quick to consume and assume almost anything that is salacious with very little consideration for or interest in the truth.

Nonetheless, our responsibility is to love all God's children regardless of what they have done to cause us setbacks, pain, or frustrations. God will convert for our good whatever the enemy intended for our destruction; pressure will be transformed into praise.

> For in the time of trouble he shall hide me in his pavilion: in the secret of his tabernacle shall he hide me; he shall set me up upon a rock. And now shall mine head be lifted up above mine enemies round about me: therefore will I offer in his tabernacle sacrifices of joy; I will sing, yea, I will sing praises unto the Lord. Hear, O Lord, when I cry with my voice: have mercy also upon me, and answer me. (Psalm 27:5–7)

> Know ye that the Lord he is God: it is he that hath made us, and not we ourselves; we are his people, and the sheep of his pasture. Enter into his gates with thanksgiving, and into his courts with praise: be thankful unto him, and bless his name. For the Lord is good; his mercy is everlasting; and his truth endureth to all generations. (Psalm 100:3–5)

And the peace of God, which passeth all understanding, shall keep your hearts and minds through Christ Jesus. Finally, brethren, whatsoever things are true, whatsoever things are honest, whatsoever things are just, whatsoever things are pure, whatsoever things are lovely, whatsoever things are of good report; if there be any virtue, and if there be any praise, think on these things. (Philippians 4:7–8)

Pain Births Blessings

Pain is one of the fundamental indicators that a pregnant woman is about to have her baby. She must prepare herself for the arrival of what is causing her so much discomfort psychologically, physically, emotionally, and spiritually for the blessings of new birth. Miraculously, after the pushing, discomfort, tears, and pain, she receives a bundle of joy and her agony dissipates. You may weep at night, but you will rejoice in the morning!

My wife and I have been blessed with three kids; I witnessed the birth of two. I was always amazing to see the joy and excitement our bundle of joy brought to my wife, notwithstanding her earlier pains and pangs of childbirth. We cried tears of joy as we proudly embraced and meticulously examined the new gift of life.

You Will Birth Something Transformational

The enemy can sense that purpose is about to be released; the pains and frustrations are just indicators that you are about to birth something transformational. Your Pharaoh will show up when your Moses is about to be born. Your Goliath will appear when your David is anointed. The enemy will always show his ugly head when your purpose is about to be fulfilled.

My last two years have been the most painful and stressful years of my life, yet they have been the most rewarding. This book was birthed as a direct result of the pain and frustration I felt as I waited for God to deliver me from the snares of those who desired my destruction. I found myself being maliciously and falsely accused of a criminal offense, subsequently plotted against politically, charged, and arrested. Only by God's intervention was I freed by a court of law without me having to utter one word in my defense. During that dark period in my life, I began to speak God's Word back to Him and remind Him what He said He would do on my behalf as His child.

As I waited for God to deal with my enemies, I reluctantly observed that He was not in any haste and that He was more concerned about me! He began to challenge my thoughts and attitudes with His Word daily, and I saw myself evolving and transitioning from focusing on my enemies to turning my attention to His purpose for my life, hence, *Transformation in the midst of Transition*.

As my mind began to be renewed daily, my attitudes and behavior transformed. I began to document lessons that I learned as I experienced a metamorphic transformation from immaturely seeking revenge to being forgiving and loving in spite of what others had done to me.

God continuously reminded me that what I was experiencing was His battle and He would get His glory out of my situation. My flesh wanted revenge, but God wanted my transformation, and He won! God began to reveal to me that my trials were designed by Him to mature me and remove my flesh so I would learn to give Him the glory and praise regardless of my situation.

> James, a servant of God and of the Lord Jesus Christ, to the twelve tribes which are scattered abroad, greeting. My brethren, count it all joy when ye fall into divers temptations; knowing this, that the trying of your faith worketh patience. (James 1:1–3)

A Transformed Attitude—Count It All Joy

As God did His work in me, I learned to thank Him in all my trials, praise Him throughout my disappointments, love my enemies, forgive myself, forgive my player-haters, and count it all joy. I gradually saw my attitudes transformed, my mind renewed, and my joy return. I was able to look my enemies in their eyes with a smile again, because God kept on reminding me it was not my battle, it was His. Often, I wanted to scream to God that I needed to say something because I needed to clear my name, but I kept on getting the same response—that this fight was not mine.

I remembered so vividly telling someone, "God will have you right here to see when He gets His glory out of this situation." I had just painfully discovered that this individual was one of the chief organizers of a malicious plot designed to undermine me and have me removed from a leadership position I held in the secular world.

Psychologically, emotionally, and physically, I was battered by this vicious attack and could no longer focus on my duties. I subsequently applied for an extended vacation, and to my surprise, I discovered I had almost a year of vacation time accumulated. During that time, I went before God seeking answers; I was broken by the pain of Judas's betrayal, bleeding from a wound inflicted by Jezebel's knife, and exhausted from trying to escape Pharaoh's army.

My wife constantly reminded me that we served a mighty God who would not allow the enemy to triumph over us. I thank God for the character He gave my wife, who demonstrated love, forgiveness, and support even when I did not deserve it. She always reminded me that she had my back and kept me covered in prayers. I found myself waking at night with tears coming down my face questioning God about what He was trying to say in the midst of my tribulation. One night, about three in the morning, I went into the bathroom and began to question Him, and I remember these words: *Son, I am transforming and transitioning you to another level.* I grabbed my notepad and pencil and began to write as God began to minister to me about what I was experiencing.

I discovered there were issues, hurts, and pains in me that had a stranglehold on my life, issues concerning rejection, pride, unforgiveness, and many psychological scars that had been festering for many years. I was a spiritual mess. I began to confess them to the Lord and seek His Word to heal me; I asked for His strength to close the doors that were left opened in my life.

Mysteriously, I began to repent of all the sins the Holy Spirit brought to my remembrance and to pray for strength to forgive. My faith began to increase, and I began to daily declare God's Word back to Him. My focus shifted from my enemies to my shortcomings and failures. My marriage needed attention and healing, my wife needed her confidant back, and my children needed their father. I had become a cold-hearted person who was concerned primarily with the success of the organization I headed at that time.

As God transformed my life, He simultaneously transitioned me to a new level where I did not think the same any longer. My goals, desires, needs, and perspectives on life changed. I progressively realized I could not continue operating in the same way after experiencing that metaphorical change. Subsequently, I left public service after twenty years, opened my own business, homeschooled our three children personally, and began pursuing God's calling for me. God began to reveal to me that He was the one who had created my enemies, and that my duty was to love them! I did not want to love those who had deliberately plotted to destroy my reputation and career. I clearly identified with what Joseph felt when his envious brothers sold him into slavery, when he was lied on by Potiphar's wife, and when he was thrown in prison. I was comforted by the fact that Joseph's process was part of his purpose. Every trial he encountered was divinely purposed to transition him toward his destiny—second in command of Egypt.

This reality motivated me to hold my peace, keep my joy, shout up, and watch God fight my battles. Yes, it was not easy to hold my peace while my enemies were having a field day with my name, sending intimidating remarks to my family, and threatening our finances. My wife and I took comfort in the scripture that assured us, "No weapon that is formed against thee shall prosper; and every tongue that shall rise against thee in judgment thou shalt condemn. This is the heritage of the servants of the LORD, and their righteousness is of me, saith the LORD" (Isaiah 54:17).

Transformation Brings Revelation

- Your Goliaths will come roaring at you when you have been anointed for greatness.
- You will defeat your Goliaths with God's help and in His way.
- Your success as a believer will attract the hatred, envy, and jealousy of your enemies who unfortunately might just be your brothers and sisters in the Lord.

- Your enemies are on assignment to push you into your destiny. Let them!
- The devil will use anyone, anything, at any time, and at any place to destroy you.
- Trust Jesus. The arms of flesh will fail you.
- Embrace the many opportunities of your storm, and allow them to refine your character.
- Hold your peace and let God fight for you because He knows how to win.
- Forgive your enemies quickly and let God be God.
- Seek cleansing, not revenge.
- Pray for your enemies and love them unconditionally regardless of what they might have done to you.
- When God overrules on your behalf, give Him the glory!

Transformation Brings Vindication

Believers' battles belong to God. God has promised in His Word that He will fight for us. Our responsibility is to be still. That does not mean not acting but being prayerful during the attacks. Our hope ought to be in the awesome power of our Lord, who can cancel our enemies' agenda and seal the mouths of the lions that seek our destruction.

The devil is an accuser of the brethren; he will use anyone you allow to penetrate your circle and carry out his evil schemes. I am so glad Jesus loves me; when my back is against the wall and I have no one to come to my defense, He steps in as my lawyer and overrules the enemies' snares.

Friend, when you trust in the Lord, the traps set to ensnare you will be overruled. The well-planned plots and craftily concocted lies will be overruled. The lions sent to consume you will be overruled. The snake sent to bite you will be overruled. The accusation designed to destroy you, your family, marriage, business, and good name will be overruled. The judge will be overruled. The obeah, the witchcraft, and the attacks on your ministry will be overruled by Christ's shed blood.

When man speaks death, God speaks life. God declares that your funeral is canceled, releases you from the chains of your enemies, and declares that whomever the Son sets free is free indeed! When God is on your side, others cannot do anything about it. Subsequently, believers should take comfort from Isaiah 41:10–14, relax, and allow God to overrule their enemies.

- Do not be afraid of your enemies.
- Remember that God is with you.
- Do not get discouraged or depressed.
- God will give you the strength to endure what you are going through.
- God will help you and uphold you with His hand of righteousness.
- Your enemies will be shamed and confounded.
- Your enemies' impact on you will be powerless, and they will perish.
- Your enemies will be nonexistent, and you will not be able to find them when God is finished with them.
- God will hold you up and be your support.
- Do not be afraid because God will help you.

> Fear thou not; for I am with thee: be not dismayed; for I am thy God: I will strengthen thee; yea, I will help thee; yea, I will uphold thee with the right hand of my righteousness. Behold, all they that were incensed against thee shall be ashamed and confounded: they shall be as nothing; and they that strive with thee shall perish. Thou shalt seek them, and shalt not find them, even them that contended with thee: they that war against thee shall be as nothing, and as a thing of nought. For I the Lord thy God will hold thy right hand, saying unto thee, Fear not; I will help thee. Fear not, thou worm Jacob, and ye men of Israel; I will help thee, saith the Lord, and thy redeemer, the Holy One of Israel. (Isaiah 41:10–14)

Transformation Brings Restoration—Take Your Licking but Come Out Ticking

Not only will God overrule your enemies, He will also restore to you everything the enemy has stolen from you. Your health, wealth, joy, peace, opportunities, smile, name, business, family, marriage—you name it—He will restore to you! When the enemy attempts to destroy your good name, remember that the God we serve has promised that His people will never be ashamed and that whatever is taken from them will be restored.

God intervened and overruled my enemies on my behalf. Ironically, God allowed that same individual whom I had told would be around when God got the glory out of my situation to actually be there. God made a divine intervention, interrupted my funeral, and snatched me out of the coffin my enemies had vindictively put me in. God restored everything to me with bonuses as those who had wanted to destroy me watched in amazement.

The bad that was experienced caused the good to be manifested in my life; my relationship with God was strengthened, my marriage blossomed, my finances were increased, my stress was reduced, and I had a book to publish.

Develop the right attitude, be honest, and seek God's face daily for the wisdom to benefit from every trial, storm, or difficulty God sanctioned you to experience. If it did not kill you, it was meant to bless you. Are you willing to learn so you can be transitioned to your next level in God?

Michelle Obama said during the 2016 presidential campaign, "When they go low, we go high." I had to learn that strategy in dealing with my enemies. They will try to bring you to their lowest levels of dirt, gossip, and slander, but you must fly like an eagle above the dark clouds. Let God do the fighting for you because He has never lost a battle. He will restore all that your envious cankerworms, locusts, palmerworms, and caterpillars have stolen.

> And the floors shall be full of wheat, and the vats shall overflow with wine and oil. And I will restore to you the years that the locust hath eaten, the cankerworm,

and the caterpiller, and the palmerworm, my great army which I sent among you. And ye shall eat in plenty, and be satisfied, and praise the name of the Lord your God that hath dealt wondrously with you: and my people shall never be ashamed. (Joel 2:24–26)

Transformation Brings Maturity

I am thankful I serve a merciful God who searches our hearts, reads our minds, and loves the unlovable. God is well able to settle your situation when others do everything they can to destroy and malign your character. Friend, God has the records in heaven and will not allow your enemy to have a field day with any of His children. The days of torment from your enemies will soon be over; just keep them in prayers as Job did when he was in trouble.

> And the Lord turned the captivity of Job, when he prayed for his friends: also the Lord gave Job twice as much as he had before. Then came there unto him all his brethren, and all his sisters, and all they that had been of his acquaintance before, and did eat bread with him in his house: and they bemoaned him, and comforted him over all the evil that the Lord had brought upon him: every man also gave him a piece of money, and everyone an earring of gold. So the Lord blessed the latter end of Job more than his beginning: for he had fourteen thousand sheep, and six thousand camels, and a thousand yoke of oxen, and a thousand she asses. He had also seven sons and three daughters. (Job 42:10–12)

Your transformation is waiting on your maturity. God is looking for you to grow spiritually from any situation He permits in your life. Complaining and feeling sorry for yourself are not the answers. God wants us to wipe our tears, straighten our backs, dust our clothes of, hold our heads up, and get in position so He can fight for us. We do that by putting our trust in His Word to work on our behalf because we cannot fight the enemy with our own strength.

> I called upon the Lord in distress: the Lord answered me, and set me in a large place. The Lord is on my side; I will not fear: what can man do unto me? The Lord taketh my part with them that help me: therefore shall I see my desire upon them that hate me. (Psalm 118:5–7)

The enemy can smell that something beautiful is ahead and will try to summon his demons to attack your job, community, and family and delay, abort, or destroy your destiny. But God's plan for your life is assured; no devil can stop it. Just count it all joy and let God transform your accusation into a celebration of His awesome power.

I have experienced the restorative power of God in my life. I have patiently learned that fire that seeks to destroy us often becomes a blessing. The fire heated seven times hotter to consume us will become bearable because we have put our trust in God, not in any justice system. The fire that cannot consume us will kill those who threw us in it. Those who ordered us into the fire will have to order us out, and our Chaldeans who accused us in the first place will be assembled to witness how God overrules and restores everything that was stolen from us. God will bring transformation in the midst of our accusations. He is with us in our darkest hours when our storms are raging, and He reassures us confidently, "I'll take you there!"

Key Points to Remember

- ✓ When God overrules, man has no say because God has the final say concerning your future, and it is not over until God says so.
- ✓ Your lions may roar at you, but they cannot touch you.
- ✓ God will overrule on our behalf and summon those who put us in our situations to come and pull us out.
- ✓ When God overrules, He shatters the plans of the enemies, frustrates their agenda, and delivers His people on time.

- ✓ God numbers the days of our enemies, and when He steps in, they will not be able to execute their malicious, wicked, and hypocritical plans.
- ✓ Love looks beyond the sin and sees the need for deliverance, forgiveness, restoration, and healing.
- ✓ God does not use your shortcomings to determine your future.
- ✓ The pressure from the storms and trials can easily leave you weak and defenseless, but God in His wisdom converts that pressure into praise.
- ✓ The enemy can sense that purpose is about to be released, and the pains and frustrations are just indicators that you are about to birth something transformational.
- ✓ Transformation will produce revelation, vindication, maturity, and restoration.
- ✓ Your Goliaths will come roaring at you when you have been anointed for greatness.
- ✓ Your success as a believer will attract the hatred, envy, and jealousy of your enemies who unfortunately might just be your brothers and sisters in the Lord.
- ✓ Your enemies are on assignment to push you into your destiny. Let them do that.
- ✓ The devil will use anyone, anything, at any time, and at any place to try to destroy you.
- ✓ God is looking for spiritual growth from any situation He permits into your life.
- ✓ If your storm did not kill you, it was meant to bless you!
- ✓ The enemy can smell that something beautiful is ahead and will try to summon all his demons to attack your job, community, and family and try to delay, abort, or destroy your destiny.
- ✓ God will bring transformation in the midst of your accusation.

CHAPTER 7

---❦---

TRANSITIONING THROUGH YOUR STORM— "I'LL TAKE YOU THERE!"

G od allows challenges and trials in our lives to help us develop the characteristics we need to fulfill His purposes on earth. The period of transition often comes packaged in the form of a storm as believers make their way to the other side toward maturity in Christ.

You may be a Christian, but you will nonetheless encounter storms. Jesus may be in your boat, but you will still encounter storms. Storms are necessary because they often come pregnant with opportunities to help strengthen, refine, and mature your faith.

As believers, we cannot choose the types of storms we experience, but we can control our responses to them, exercise patience in their midst, and trust God While we ride out our storms. The purpose for the storms is not always easily identifiable, but opportunities for spiritual development are always there for learning.

Some storms were released to transition your Christian faith from fearing the storm to being capable of actually walking through the storm. God wants to transition you from a position of fear to faith, from being a storm rider to being a storm walker. God is devotedly aware that you are in a storm, so do not ignore, despise, or trivialize the storm that was sent to propel you closer to your destiny. Your storms are often seasoned with purpose and unrecognizable blessings; your Deliverer can come to your rescue in the very storm that troubles you the most.

And the same day, when the even was come, he saith unto them, Let us pass over unto the other side. And when they had sent away the multitude, they took him even as he was in the ship. And there were also with him other little ships. And there arose a great storm of wind, and the waves beat into the ship, so that it was now full. And he was in the hinder part of the ship, asleep on a pillow: and they awake him, and say unto him, Master, carest thou not that we perish? And he arose, and rebuked the wind, and said unto the sea, Peace, be still. And the wind ceased, and there was a great calm. And he said unto them, why are ye so fearful? How is it that ye have no faith? And they feared exceedingly, and said one to another, what manner of man is this, that even the wind and the sea obey him? (Mark 4:35–41)

Our Unexpected Storms

Our storms can come with very little warning; that is God's way of discovering what is in our hearts. Like a master teacher, He often withdraws to observe our responses and determine whether we have learned the lesson and prepared for the next level He has predestined for us. We may be within God's will and obey His command to go to the other side but still experience storms because storms come to us all.

We can predict natural storms to a degree, but our spiritual storms can take us by surprise and make us think they were designed to take us out. Nevertheless, please remember that Captain Jesus will pilot our boats through any storm. He attended the best spiritual navigation institute and graduated at the head of His class. He is so confident in storms that He is known to have slept through storms; if you wake Him up, He simply speaks a word to the wind and the waves, and they listen to Him. He is so good that He walks on water; if you have enough faith, He will allow you to do that too. Captain Jesus is so good that He reads the weather well in advance and navigates His passengers through their storms enabling them to arrive safely to the other side. All He insists on is for you to put your trust in Him and do not be afraid. When you get anxious and worried as you transition through your storm, He comforts you with a calm assurance, "I will take you there!"

The Calm before the Storm

Jesus had just concluded a very long and exhausting day of preaching from a boat due to the very large crowd of people when He gave the instruction, "Let us pass over to the other side." Perhaps all the disciples were beat from the extended evangelical initiative and were happy to be refreshed by a relaxing cruise. The water was just right; Jesus could not have chosen a better time to travel across the inviting, rejuvenating, and calming water.

We believers are often exhausted by the cares of this world right when Jesus asks us to go on a journey with Him. Quite naturally, we comply since the Master will be accompanying us. The spiritual reality is that even though our Savior is with us as we reposition ourselves to the other side, we are not exempt from experiencing stormy weather.

The calm before the storm should not deceive us into believing our lives are without stormy seas. Our faith ought to be tested every now and again to see how well we can apply what we have learned. Storms are therefore great opportunities to put our faith on trial. What will you do under such circumstances? How will you respond to such trials? A faith that is not tested is one that cannot be trusted.

Transformational Lessons from a Storm

One of the main purposes of storms in our lives is to test our faith to see how much spiritual maturity we have. The main goal of our storm is to reveal the real us without layers of religiosity and spiritual gymnastics; we see as if in a mirror all our strengths and weaknesses.

There are critical lessons to learn from our storms.

- **Obedience does not exempt you from a storm.** Obedience to God's command does not exempt you from trials and tribulations. Jesus told His disciples they were going to the other side, but they encountered a storm. Likewise, you may be in obedience to what you know God has approved, yet you will encounter a storm because storms are necessary for our spiritual growth and maturity.

- **Having Jesus with you does not exempt you from a storm**. The disciples were accompanied by Jesus but still encountered a storm. Jesus will be with you in your storms in your church, ministry, home, marriage, job, business, and elsewhere.
- **Doing the will of God does not exempt you from a storm**. The disciples were doing the will of God, yet they experienced a storm. The work of the Lord will not exempt Christians from experiencing storms.
- **Storms come to us all**. The disciples realized that none of them was exempted from the storms. The storm did not exempt the most spiritual or most anointed. The same storm that Peter experienced was the same one Judas did. Rich and poor, black and white, educated and uneducated, all will experience storms because they come to everyone.

The Purpose of the Storm

Each storm God allows believers to experience has a specific assignment—to test or strengthen their faith, push them closer to their destinies, or redirect them back to God.

Jesus knows all our storms including those we will face in the future. He designs and carefully selects our storms that are pregnant with opportunities for our faith to be enhanced, but it is up to us to accept the lessons of the storms and apply them to our lives.

Jesus accompanies us through all our storms like a father. Ironically, He appears asleep often just to observe how we will react and function in the midst of our storms according to Mark 4:38–41. The disciples learned quickly that Jesus was with them in their storm though they thought He was asleep. Many Christians may think Jesus is asleep because He appears not to be cognizant of what is happening to them. How wrong they are; the Captain Himself approved the storms in the first place! He is patiently waiting to see who will demonstrate faith in dealing with the storm. He is looking for maturity through the application of all that is in His Word. The quicker we learn that God is with us and can handle any occasion, the better we will be able to acknowledge our storms are times for us to demonstrate what we have learned so we can transition to our next level.

I grew up on the tranquil island of Cat Island, one of the easterly islands of the Bahamas. Due to the island's proximity to the ocean, it is usually impacted by the remnants of hurricanes, tropical storms, and other severe weather systems. After storms, people knew that they could profit by finding what the storm had blown in—lumber, rope, containers, and every now and then a small dinghy. As you may imagine, the policy was you kept what you found. The storms also took away sand, recreated the landscape of the shore, and removed debris.

Likewise, your spiritual storms can bring blessings and opportunities for growth and wash away attitudinal junk, pride, hypocrisy, self-righteousness, judgmental behavior, fear, doubt, disobedience, arrogance, immaturity, faithlessness, and self-reliance. In essence, your storms will expose the real you to you. You will realize that you are not so super spiritual after all and that you still have something to learn if only humility.

Storms can have different purposes.

- **To redirect a believer to an aborted assignment.** We are told in scriptures how a storm transitioned a disobedient Jonah back to His God whose assignment he had tried to run away from. Some storms have a divine assignment to navigate those of us who may be disobedient from time to time back to our purpose and destiny in God. We can run, but we cannot hide.

- **To direct one to new witnessing opportunities.** Paul experienced a storm with a different assignment—to transition him to where he would get additional opportunities to minister as he made his way to Rome for his trial. This storm shows that we do not need to fear our storms because God sometimes uses situations we may consider unfair and terrible and converts them into blessings. This type of storm teaches us to trust God and allow Him to get His glory out of our lives. This storm will transition us into the presence of our destinies.

- **To strengthen and build believers' faith.** Most important, another type of storm is design to build believers' faith. This storm was the one the disciples experienced. Jesus, the Captain, was concerned that His crew needed a crash course in faith, so He meticulously designed and sanctioned a storm to transition their faith higher. He wanted them to acknowledge that they needed to put their trust in Him and not panic when the waves of life were threatening their boat.
  - First, He wanted them to understand that sometimes, they might be doing what He told them to do, but they still would encounter storms.
  - Second, Jesus might seem asleep during their storms, but they ought to be aware He would not allow anything bad to happen to them.
  - Third, the disciples should not be intimidated by the wind and the waves that threatened their boat for they could be stilled.
  - Fourth, He wanted them to see where their faith really was and to challenge their faith to come up higher.
  - Fifth, He had the power to calm any storm that troubled them, and He wanted to demonstrate how they were to handle a storm after it had fulfilled its purpose: "Peace! Be still!"

Tests and trials are often very good indicators of our mastery of the skills necessary to transition to the next level. The believers' faith is tested regularly to determine their growth and maturity in God. Often in life, we think we have it all together until a problem comes and we find ourselves like Peter did denying our Master a short time after we promised Him total allegiance.

"I Will Take You There!"

Jesus assures us He will take us through all of life's stormy seas. Like the disciples, we may be amazed how He does what He does and ask, "What manner of man is this?" Jesus will take us over treacherous waves and through billowing winds to where He wants us to be. He will go with us, and He is always ready and able to tackle any unexpected situation we may encounter.

Jesus will keep us safe and provide shelter in the midst of our storms. He kept us safe when the devil thought he had us and even when we thought the devil had us! The Christian's journey is safe with Jesus. There are many opportunities and blessings hidden in the midst of the storms that each believer ought to embrace.

Embracing the Opportunities of Your Storm

Christians can go through what we are going through, knowing that our storms come filled with opportunities to transform and mature our faith to a point where we trust God completely. Our flesh often interferes with our spiritual development, but we will have so many opportunities to prosper from the storms and trials we go through. Our storms and trials are filled with spiritual benefits, and we can prosper in any storm.

- Storms can provide witnessing opportunities (Acts 27, 28).
- Storms can help you to see God more clearly than you have before (Jonah 1:15–16).
- Storms can cause your testimony to help further the gospel (Philippians 1:12–13).
- Storms can strengthen your character (Romans 5:3–4).
- Storms can cause the Lord to be exalted in your life (Philippians 1:19–21).
- Storms will help you to know Christ in a deeper way (Philippians 3:10).
- Storms can help you focus on the future and leave the past in the past (Philippians 3:13–14; 2 Corinthians 5:17).
- Storms can teach you how to totally depend and trust God and Him alone (Job 1:19–22).
- Storms can usher you into a new level of financial blessings (Job 42:10–13).
- Storms can teach us how to be humble (Philippians 2:3–4).
- Storms can teach you dependence on God to provide for all your needs (Philippians 4:19).

- Storms can teach you to have peace in all circumstances (Philippians 4:10–14).
- Storms can teach you to focus on the greater reward (2 Corinthians 4:16–18, 5:1–2).
- Storms can teach you how to be kind to one another (Galatians 6:1–5).
- Storms can make you battle ready and stronger than you were before (Galatians 6:9–10).
- Storms can strengthen you spiritually (2 Corinthians 12:9–10).
- Storms can strengthen your faith (1 Peter 1:6–7).
- Storms can develop your patience (James 1:2–4).
- Storms can teach you that God is your protector (Psalm 27:5, 32:7).
- Storms can teach you how to cry out to God (Psalm 34:6, 17).
- Storms can teach you that God is your refuge and strength (Psalm 46:1–3, 59:16).

The Power of a Storm

The storm intended to break you can very well make you. God is looking for complete transformational change, and often, He allows storms to propel believers toward their destinies. Storms are ripe with transformational opportunities for maturity. You can emerge from them strengthened by your faith and relying more on God.

A storm can test your spiritual stamina. Trials and troubles will reveal your character, whom you trust, and whom you are depending on. They will challenge your ability to trust God, love and forgive your enemies, have joy, peace, longsuffering, patience, and endurance in the midst of your storm.

Jesus saw the disciples not applying their faith to the storm and questioned their faith. Believers often have faith but are lacking in their ability to apply it. Storms give believers opportunities to demonstrate their faith. What you learn during your personal time with God ought to be used tangibly against the enemy. You can command your mornings to line up and produce fruitfulness because as a believer, you have the power to proclaim life or death over your situation.

Believers' spiritual vulnerabilities and insecurities are brought to light during their troubles. The storms will reveal just how much they value their lives and how much sacrifice they are willing to make for the gospel. The areas of their lives that needs strengthening and spiritual pruning are revealed during trials, and it is their responsibility to seek God's face to fortify their weaknesses.

Storms help us realign our priorities and refocus our goals toward our destinies rather than toward our selfish, meaningless ambitions. Trials can cause us to reflect on our lives and determine what went wrong. During this time of self-examination, we can prayerfully ask God to have His way and be our only Captain who will take us through blustering winds, tempestuous waves, and threatening shoals.

Life and troubles are seasonal; they are like the tides. Experience has taught me not to panic in my troubles because after their purpose is fulfilled, they will pass. Sometimes, life serves hot days, cold days, and stormy days, but we can be assured that the weather will change. We can transition through our storms; our Shepherd will lead us to the path of righteousness.

> The Lord is my shepherd; I shall not want. He maketh me to lie down in green pastures: he leadeth me beside the still waters. He restoreth my soul: he leadeth me in the paths of righteousness for his name's sake. Yea, though I walk through the valley of the shadow of death, I will fear no evil: for thou art with me; thy rod and thy staff they comfort me. Thou preparest a table before me in the presence of mine enemies: thou anointest my head with oil; my cup runneth over. Surely goodness and mercy shall follow me all the days of my life: and I will dwell in the house of the Lord forever. (Psalm 23)

Your storm that looked like a setback was positioning you for a transformation. The storm that seemed as if it were meant to break you was divinely orchestrated to prepare you to fulfill your destiny. Your trials and troubles were purposefully anointed to usher you closer to your destiny. Subsequently, they should not be despised but ought to be embraced with the assurance the apostle Paul had knowing you may have been shipwrecked on purpose!

Key Points to Remember

- ✓ You may be a Christian, but you will still encounter storms.
- ✓ Storms are often pregnant with opportunities to help strengthen, refine, and mature your faith.
- ✓ God wants to transition you from a position of fear to faith, from being a storm rider to becoming a storm walker.
- ✓ Obedience does not exempt you from storms.
- ✓ Doing the will of God does not exempt you from storms.
- ✓ Your storm is on a divine assignment to redirect you, to create new opportunities for witnessing, and to strengthen and enhance your faith.
- ✓ We must discover the purposes for our storms.
- ✓ Your storms are filled with opportunities to transform and mature your faith and to transition you to a point that you trust God completely and exclusively.
- ✓ Embrace the opportunities inherent in your storms.
- ✓ Sometimes, life serves hot days, cold days, and stormy days, but that will always change.
- ✓ Believers' spiritual vulnerabilities and insecurities are often exposed during their troubles.
- ✓ The areas of believers' lives that needs strengthening and spiritual pruning are revealed during trials, and they must seek God's face to fortify their weaknesses.
- ✓ The storm intended to break you can very well be the storm that makes you.
- ✓ Storms are powerful and saturated with transformational opportunities for maturity.
- ✓ Your storm that looked like a setback was positioning you for a transformational comeback!
- ✓ Your trials and troubles were purposefully anointed to usher you closer to your destiny.

CHAPTER 8

...—⚘—...

TRANSFORMATIVE POWER OF A STORM— SHIPWRECKED ON PURPOSE

One of the many wonderful attributes about God is that He can allow storms in our lives that have a divine assignment, which is to point us towards our destinies. God often allows storms to rearrange our spiritual surroundings and break the human chains that limit our influence, ministry, productivity, and ability to fulfill our destinies.

Storms can change our perspective; we can see them as God's way of transitioning us into the next level of our destiny. My friend, could it be that our shipwrecks as believers are often times intentional?

God knows what is best for His children, and He is busy working out His purposes in their lives. God has planned the believers' future. Everything that happens to them were known and approved by God.

Do Not Despise Your Storm—It Is God's Action Plan

What look like storms and problems are often God's action plan to transition you into your destiny. You may think you are thriving spiritually, financially, emotionally, and purposefully, but God has greater blessings planned for you. Quite often, your spiritual landscape is too small and your vision is blurry due to the many obstacles in your present position. Your problems are therefore individually crafted and handpicked by God to transition you to a place where God's agenda would be pursued. Do not despise your trials; God specializes in creating storms to anoint, bless, and promote you into your destiny. God has a reason for all your trials. You have to trust His timing because He is always on time whereas your timing is usually selfish, fleshly, and egotistic.

Remember these three key points in the midst of your storm:

1. **God has your best interest at heart, and He has good plans for you.** "For I know the thoughts that I think toward you, saith the LORD, thoughts of peace, and not of evil, to give you an expected end" (Jeremiah 29:11).
2. **God is busy working things out in your favor.** "And we know that all things work together for good to them that love God, to them who are the called according to his purpose" (Romans 8:28).
3. **Trust God because His timing is always beautiful.** "He hath made everything beautiful in his time: also he hath set the world in their heart, so that no man can find out the work that God maketh from the beginning to the end" (Ecclesiastes 3:11).

A Storm of Destiny

The apostle Paul was battered by a ferocious storm, shipwrecked, had to swim to save his life, and was attacked by a poisonous snake, but his destiny was assured. You may be shattered too by the storms of life, left shipwrecked in places and around people you do not know, but God has you right where you are supposed to be! Your responsibility is to bloom regardless of where you are.

God wants to reposition you to a place where you can depend only on Him. He wants to destroy the ship you have been depending on for many years—you know, that stuff that you paid all your attention to, yes the thing you worshiped so much that God could not get His glory out of you. For me, it was my job. I was a workaholic who put work above Him and my family for many years, but I am so glad He redirected my focus just in time. God will allow a storm to get your attention because His purpose for your life should always be your priority.

I have had storms in my marriage, job, businesses, and more recently, with cancer. Amazingly, they all came pregnant with a purpose to propel me closer to my destiny. My ship, my body I had depended on to work hard and provide for my family, could no longer cope with the stress of chemotherapy, but God wanted me to know that my job was not my source of worth—He was. God protected me in the midst of my medical storm, and I learned to trust Him more.

Additionally, I started a war-room approach to praying; I led my family in prayers every morning during my twelve months of chemotherapy. As you may imagine, there were many difficult days when I did not feel thankful, or prayerful, but God honored my commitment and allowed me to develop patience and perseverance in the midst of that storm. I learned how to thank God in the midst of my pain, frustration, and chemo treatments. I learned God was transforming my mind to trust Him and preparing me spiritually for the transition to a new level of praise.

I remember vividly sitting on a Thanksgiving Day at my oncologist's office in Nassau, Bahamas, watching the Thanksgiving parade on television as I underwent chemo. I patiently listened to many horrifying stories of others' battles with cancer, and I realized I was still blessed, and had every right to give God the glory just because I was alive. Often, I closed my eyes and silently thanked God for all His goodness toward me in spite of my condition.

Surprisingly, nearly four hours later, I was usually awakened by a nurse tapping my hands to tell me I was all done. I would happily rush to the airport to catch a short flight back to the Berry Islands, another island in the Bahamas, where I lived. In spite of the many challenges experienced during my yearlong travels for treatment, I developed a hunger for more of God and a deeper appreciation for my family. I watched with tearful eyes how my wife and kids would do all they could to help make me as comfortable as they could, and my love for them grew immensely.

During my recovery from surgery and subsequent battle with colon cancer, I discovered how God could get my attention in a storm and redirect my attention from the storm to the many rainbows in them. I realized I could live through my pain and pray through my storms because they were all working for my good. God expanded my vison to see the bigger picture of what He was transforming in my life. I have been strengthened and refined by my storms; I learned God still specializes in what others say is impossible.

Many times, Christians can become complacent and comfortable in our present seasons assuming we have arrived, but God has a more profound plan for us. Ministry is imbedded in us, but often, it would not be resurrected had it not been for the trials and storms that pushed us to our knees to seek the protection and provision of God.

Some Storms Are Anointed to Redirect Our Vision

Regularly, God will send a storm to redirect believers' vision toward His purposes and agenda for a season. Sometimes, the many successes and accolades they receive can mislead them into believing that success has been attained and God is satisfied. As a result, the undiscovered land is left unoccupied, the giants are unchallenged, and the Philistines are left to defy the true and living God.

> And there the centurion found a ship of Alexandria sailing into Italy; and he put us therein. And when we had sailed slowly many days, and scarce were come over against Cnidus, the wind not suffering us, we sailed under Crete, over against Salmone; and, hardly passing it, came unto a place which is called the fair havens; nigh whereunto was the city of Lasea. Now when much time was spent, and when sailing was now dangerous, because the fast was now already past, Paul admonished them, and said unto them, Sirs, I perceive that this voyage will be with hurt and much damage, not only of the lading and ship, but also of our lives. Nevertheless the centurion believed the master and the owner of the ship, more than those things which were spoken by Paul. And because the haven was not commodious to winter in, the more part advised to depart thence also, if by any means they might attain to Phenice, and there to winter; which is an haven of Crete, and lieth toward the south west and north west. (Acts 27:6–12)

Paul discerned that the journey to Rome would be dangerous; he made his feelings known but to no avail. Sometimes, destiny calls, and we cannot shun our purpose regardless how dangerous our journeys may be. Our hope and trust ought to be anchored in Jesus, who can give us peace even in the midst of a storm. The path to destiny may be treacherous and unpredictable, but God will protect His purpose and investment.

Some Storms Are Designed to Attack Your Ship

As God transitions us into our new seasons, we instinctively cling to the safety of our accustomed ships—our jobs, careers, businesses, income generators, ministries, and talents. Often, God sanctions a storm designed to propel us to another level in Him, but we defiantly and religiously use our energies and efforts to preserve and hold onto the *ships* God is patiently trying to disconnect from our lives.

God wants you to recognize Him not any of your *ships* as your true source. Your relationships, friendships, leaderships, mentorships, and Companionships, all should be submitted to God. Your reliance and dependence on earthly sustenance cannot bring satisfaction because you were not meant to live on bread alone.

> And when the south wind blew softly, supposing that they had obtained their purpose, loosing thence, they sailed close by Crete. But not long after there arose against it a tempestuous wind, called Euroclydon. And when the ship was caught, and could not bear up into the wind, we let her drive. And running under a certain island which is called Clauda, we had much work to come by the boat: Which when they had taken up, they used helps, undergirding the ship; and, fearing lest they should fall into the quick sands, strake sail, and so were driven. And we being exceedingly tossed with a tempest, the next day they lightened the ship; and the third day we cast out with our own hands the tackling of the ship. (Acts 27:13–19)

Your Storm Has a Purpose

A divine purpose is attached to every trial and problem we Christians face. We can often think that the calm in our lives means we have arrived, but like Paul, we soon discover that God has a more profound plan for us. Regularly, it is another storm to transition us to another level, and simultaneously allow us to help others who desperately need our unique gifts and transformational anointing.

Friend, no one can do what God has ordained you to do, and millions of people may be waiting for you to step into your purpose and pursue your destiny. You do not even know what you are pregnant with. Let the gift you carry make room for you. Your finances perhaps are not in order because you have been reluctant to allow your storm of not enough to propel you into a new place of faith and worship in which you give God all you have. You hold onto your small loaf of bread and two small fishes rather than giving them to God. Friend, that mentality will limit your blessings and prevent others from being blessed as well. Your storm is meant to get you where you have been destined to be, and the ship you are presently on has fulfilled its purpose.

Do Not Try to Preserve What God Is Trying to Release You From

Let that ship go! Many times, we spend too much time, energy, and resources in a desperate attempt to preserve our ships that we think we need for our survival, but God is telling us to let them go. We often hold onto our impressive titles, illustrious positions, and responsible safety nets, but God is telling us we do not need that stuff in the new season He is ushering us into.

Our former seasons needed such things, but our new seasons need faith. It is transformational when we acknowledge that releasing some stuff from our ships is not good enough. Throwing away some personal belongings and the tacking of our *ships* are not enough because God wants those *ships* that we put our trust in to be wrecked and ultimately destroyed so that He alone will get the glory. The quicker we realize this, as Paul did, the sooner we will allow God to destroy them.

And when neither sun nor stars in many days appeared, and no small tempest lay on us, all hope that we should be saved was then taken away. But after long abstinence Paul stood forth in the midst of them, and said, Sirs, ye should have hearkened unto me, and not have loosed from Crete, and to have gained this harm and loss. And now I exhort you to be of good cheer: for there shall be no loss of any man's life among you, but of the ship. For there stood by me this night the angel of God, whose I am, and whom I serve, Saying, Fear not, Paul; thou must be brought before Caesar: and, lo, God hath given thee all them that sail with thee. Wherefore, sirs, be of good cheer: for I believe God, that it shall be even as it was told me. Howbeit we must be cast upon a certain island. (Acts 27:20–26)

You will not die if you release your ship because your destiny is assured by God. He is patiently waiting for your total submission to His divine plan for you.

Before I formed thee in the belly I knew thee; and before thou camest forth out of the womb I sanctified thee, and I ordained thee a prophet unto the nations. (Jeremiah 1:5)

No weapon that is formed against thee shall prosper; and every tongue that shall rise against thee in judgment thou shalt condemn. This is the heritage of the servants of the Lord, and their righteousness is of me, saith the Lord. (Isaiah 54:17)

Remember these, O Jacob and Israel; for thou art my servant: I have formed thee; thou art my servant: O Israel, thou shalt not be forgotten of me. (Isaiah 44:21)

God Wants to Get You There His Way

Life can become frustrating and unfulfilling when we don't spiritually understand our storms. Too often, what is sent to correct, direct, and instruct us we view with fleshly intention. God is still in control; He has a plan to get us where He wants us to be. Our job is to follow His map prayerfully and trust Him so we can discover our purpose in Him. God knows exactly how to transition us to the place He needs us to be in His way, on His timing, and using His methods.

Paul understood the spiritual significance of his storm. He acknowledged they had begun to celebrate prematurely; God was purposefully sending that storm. Paul took the leadership in spite of his condition as a prisoner.

God often puts us in situations so our faith can rise and be put to work. Storms are meant to strengthen our faith, and that happens when we experience challenging tasks that force our faith into action. Paul realized that it was the time and season for the glory of God to be revealed through him, but his chains had him suppressed.

Some Storms Are Designed to Break the Chains That Suppress Us

Paul was pursuing his destiny, but he was in chains. Too often, men and women of God find ourselves doing the will of God but are chained and attached to ships that have already fulfilled their purposes. It is dangerous spiritually to be chained to one season when God is transitioning us to another and we do not comprehend the timing of our storms. Failure to distinguish the spiritual relevance of our storms can leave us clinging to yesterday rather than anticipating tomorrow.

Many people are chained to traditions, ancestral curses, faithlessness, hopelessness, relationships, friendships, and leadership positions when God is trying to break up those ships so they can be free to look after His purpose. Paul's chains suppressed his freedom because he was physically chained to his ship. He was subsequently released with the other prisoners so they could swim to land. It is amazing how God can use our situation or storm to bring deliverance to many others simultaneously! The storm that was sent to attack our ministries could possibly be to set us in new ministry opportunities but also to free others around us. God is yet so awesome!

Some Storms Are Intended to Realign You with Your Destiny

Paul's storm transitioned him into his destiny. The storm that destroyed his ship could not kill him because it was only God's transportation to get him to his next season.

The many trials and storms believers encounter are usually their transport to another level of faith and new witnessing opportunities. They will know it was God because what was capable of destroying them was used to bless them and all those who were connected to them.

> And when they had taken up the anchors, they committed themselves unto the sea, and loosed the rudder bands, and hoised up the mainsail to the wind, and made toward shore. And falling into a place where two seas met, they ran the ship aground; and the forepart stuck fast, and remained unmoveable, but the hinder part was broken with the violence of the waves. And the soldiers' counsel was to kill the prisoners, lest any of them should swim out, and escape. But the centurion, willing to save Paul, kept them from their purpose; and commanded that they which could swim should cast themselves first into the sea, and get to land: And the rest, some on boards, and some on broken pieces of the ship. And so it came to pass, that they escaped all safe to land. (Acts 27:40–44)

Shipwrecked on Purpose

Setbacks, trials, obstacles, storms, and problems that can strengthen or unsettle your faith in God may interrupt your journey towards your destiny.

Just as Joseph and Paul did, many believers will have to come to the realization that God has sanctioned all the many circumstances they encounter on the pathway to destiny as divine vehicles. Every storm is tailored to transport Christians from their prisons to their palaces.

What you are pregnant with is too important to be abandoned prematurely. The baby that continues to kick on your inside needs to be nurtured and develop to full maturity. Often, like the Virgin Mary, God may have to transition you to go higher to a level of Judah (praise) until what you are pregnant with is fully matured. The many storms you came through will solidify your faith in God and nourish your potential. Someone is waiting on your testimony about how God protected you from what could have killed you. Do not give up and give in to the many trials and storms of life because God has you covered, and He will never give up on you.

My friend, do not allow what was intended to bless and promote you to cause you to lose hope and give up on God. The storms of your life will all work together for your advantage. Do not allow menacing waves and blistering winds to intimidate you. Be still and seek God's direction when the storms are raging in your life.

The enemy will always oppose your purpose, but God is depending on you to pursue the destiny He has established for you. You will know when you get there because your snake will be there to welcome you and your enemy will always show its ugly head when you are fulfilling your purpose, but like Paul, you can just shake your snake into the fire.

Key Points to Remember

- ✓ God knows what is best for His children, and He is busy working out His purposes in their lives.
- ✓ What often looks like a storm or a problem is usually God's action plan to transition you into your destiny.
- ✓ Our personal timing is usually selfish, fleshly, and egotistical, but God's timing is purposeful.
- ✓ Do not despise your trials because God specializes in creating storms that will bless, transform, and promote you into your destiny.

✓ Many times as Christians, we tend to become so complacent and comfortable in our present seasons that we assume we have arrived, but God always has a more profound plan for our existence

✓ Ministry is imbedded in us, but often, it would never have been resurrected had it not been for the trials and storms that pushed us to our knees to seek God's protection and provision.

✓ There is a divine purpose attached to every trial and problem we Christians face.

✓ Your storm is anointed to transition you into a new place, another level, and around a different group of people who desperately need your unique gifts and transformational anointing.

✓ No one can do what God has ordained and purposed you to do, so millions of people may be waiting for you to step into your purpose and pursue your destiny.

✓ Life can become frustrating and unfulfilled when you do not spiritually understand your storms.

✓ Some storms are designed to break the chains that suppress you.

✓ Many people are chained to traditions, ancestral curses, faithlessness, hopelessness, relationships, friendships, and leadership positions when God is trying to break up those ships so they can be free to look after His purpose.

✓ The many trials and storms believers encounter are usually their transport to get their faith to another level, strengthen their prayer lives, deepen their faith, and expose them to new witnessing opportunities.

✓ The storms of your life will work together for your advantage.

✓ Do not give up and give in to the many trials and storms of life because God has you covered, and He will never give up on you.

✓ Your shipwreck was on purpose!

Printed in the United States
By Bookmasters